THE WHOLE EARTH COOKBOOK

THE WHOLE EARTH COOKBOOK

Over 170 imaginative and easy-to-prepare recipes

Hilary Meth

VERMILION
LONDON

1 3 5 7 9 10 8 6 4 2

Text copyright (c) Hilary Meth 1994

The right of Hilary Meth to be identified as the author of this book has been asserted by her in accordance with the Copyright, Designs and Patents Act, 1988.

All rights reserved. No part of this publication may be reproduced, stored in a retrieval system, or transmitted in any form or by any means, electronic, mechanical, photocopying, recording or otherwise, without prior permission of the copyright owner.

First published in the United Kingdom in 1994 by Vermilion
an imprint of Ebury Press
Random House
20 Vauxhall Bridge Road
London SW1V 2SA

Random House Australia (Pty) Limited
20 Alfred Street, Milsons Point, Sydney,
New South Wales 2061, Australia

Random House New Zealand Limited
18 Poland Road, Glenfield
Auckland 10, New Zealand

Random House South Africa (Pty) Limited
PO Box 337, Bergvlei, South Africa

Random House Canada
1265 Aerowood Drive, Mississauga,
Ontario L4W 1B9

Random House UK Limited Reg. No. 954009

A CIP catalogue for this book is available from the British Library.

ISBN: 0 09 178598 7

Typeset by Textype Typesetters, Cambridge

Printed and bound in Great Britain by Cox &Wyman Ltd, Reading, Berkshire

The paper in this book is recycled and acid free.

Contents

Acknowledgements	6
Introduction	7
Foreword by Craig Sams	8
Why no added sugar?	10
Why no hydrogenated fat?	11
Why organic?	14
Why vegan?	16
How to read a label	17
Some notes on ingredients and measures	19
How to make soya yogurt	21
Recipes	
Starters	23
Hot soups	36
Chilled soups	44
Salads	46
Main courses	57
Vegetable side dishes	90
Desserts	100
Biscuits, sweets, cakes and other treats	121
Drinks	146
Menu ideas	151
Where to find the products mentioned in this book	155
Further reading	156
Index	157

Acknowledgements

I would like to thank the following people for their help: my mother, Isabel, for inspiring so many of the recipes and with Lee and Claude Frankel, a love of good food. Craig Sams and Simon Wright of Whole Earth Foods Limited for insight and support throughout the project. My agent, Jane Conway-Gordon, for help well beyond the call of duty. Fiona MacIntyre, Joanna Sheehan, Michelle Clark, and Tessa Strickland of Ebury Press for guiding and editing the project. Barbara Hughes, Kate Pemberton and Ailsa Walters for typing the manuscript. And to those who offered ideas, recipes and support in many ways: Charlotte Ambrose, Joan Bovarnick, Lucy Britton, Simonetta Calderini, Delia Cortese, Josephine Fairley, Caroline Fitzgibbons of the Soil Association, Robert Fowler, Pamela Hardyment, Christine Huggins, Scott Lauer, Michael Lavington, Sarah Peers, Janie Price, Peter Shepherd and Jennifer Weisberg.

Introduction

I approached Whole Earth with the idea of writing their cookery book because of a sort of love affair I had with their label. For years I had been seeking out their exquisitely-flavoured pure fruit jams and fresh-roasted peanut butter, just as I would travel miles for a tin of green peppercorns or straw mushrooms.

Now, they have a large range of no added sugar, vegan and organic products that stand on their own as convenience foods, but also act as raw materials for the wholefood cook. The following recipes are all without added sugar, vegan in principle (with some dairy conversions) and, hopefully, honest. This is not a book to get you to buy products just for the sake of it; the ingredients have to make a vital contribution to the taste of a recipe or the convenience of making it to have been included. There are a lot of instant recipes — both for dinner parties and every day — designed to provide a meal with the minimum of fuss. Ranging from modern English to Greek, Czech and Georgian, there are representatives of over 20 regional cuisines. Of the 170 recipes, there is a wide choice for those on all types of special diets. However, good-tasting food was the priority. Hopefully you will agree that no corners have been cut where taste is concerned, and that doing without eggs and sugar is not the hardship it first seems.

HILARY METH

Foreword

When we opened a macrobiotic restaurant in Notting Hill in West London, it became one of the trendy spots of the late 1960s, with people like the Stones, the Beatles and Terence Stamp as regulars. When people weren't making jokes about 'brown rice and sandals', they would ask how long we thought it would last, and what we would do when the wholefood fad had passed.

Our founding principles were mostly about exclusion: we banned sugar, animal products, refined foods or anything artificial. However, this outward negativity opened the doors to a blossoming creativity, as we developed new ways of enjoying foods like organic whole grains and vegetables in a variety of recipes, gleaned from the traditional cuisines of the world. Within a year, we had opened a retail shop specializing in a variety of whole foods that had never before all been available under one roof. The shop's success led to a growing wholesale business, supplying these foods to the other shops that were beginning to open all over Britain and Europe in the 1970s. We went from introducing healthy foods, like brown rice, wholemeal pasta, and wholemeal bread, to providing the sauces and spreads to accompany them, and the Whole Earth range was born.

We have never wavered from our founding principles; all Whole Earth products reflect the same integrity and commitment to quality that inspired our efforts right at the beginning.

Being unrefined and 100 per cent natural has not been enough for us, though. Food is one of life's greatest pleasures — it should be enjoyed. A product that carries the Whole Earth name has to taste delicious. So, when Hilary Meth told us that her recipes always came out well when she used Whole Earth products as ingredients, we were understandably pleased.

In the relatively few years since Whole Earth was founded, people's understanding about truly good food has changed more than ever before. There is a growing awareness of the importance to health of a high-fibre, low-sugar, low-fat diet based on unrefined, wholesome ingredients. At Whole Earth, we take heart from this great transformation. There has never been such a wide variety of superb,

FOREWORD

quality food available, produced by people around the World who are committed to restoring a natural balance and to building on the foundation of an organic way of eating to create an organic way of living on Earth. Of course, there are also more burger bars and fast food joints than ever! This is because fast food is so convenient. We hope the quick and easy recipes in *The Whole Earth Cookbook* will help to further shift the balance towards healthier eating.

CRAIG SAMS
Chairman
Whole Earth Foods

Why No Added Sugar?

Refined sugar acts like a drug in our bodies. It contains fast-acting glucose, which goes straight into the bloodstream, raising the blood sugar level and making us feel as if we have more energy. The normal level of glucose in the blood is 5 grammes, or 2 teaspoons, in your *entire* bloodstream. So, a sugary drink can triple or quadruple your blood sugar level in minutes.

Your body reacts by flooding the bloodstream with insulin to bring the glucose level down to normal. After a while, the blood sugar level is safe, but the insulin is still there, taking the level below normal. Then, you feel tired, maybe even a little depressed, hungry and crave more sugar. The stressful see-saw starts all over again. White and brown sugar, honey and maple syrup all act this way on the body. The addiction, which can be mild or severe, weakens the immune system and can lead to diabetes.

There are slower acting sweeteners that are digested as food and do not 'hit' the bloodstream as directly as sugar. Grain syrups contain maltose, which is slowly converted to glucose in the intestines. They also contain some vitamins and minerals to help in their digestion, unlike sugar, which depletes the body's reserves of these nutrients. Also, apple juice concentrate, which is high in fructose, acts more slowly and is converted into glucose as it is needed, in the body.

Artificial sweeteners, such as saccharine and aspartame, have been shown to cause cancer or neural problems in laboratory animals. The World Health Organization has set a limit of 2.5 ml/kg per day. Many soft drinks, ice lollies, jellies — traditional children's food — contain added sweeteners that, if several of those items are eaten in one day, could easily exceed this limit. Artificial sweeteners are added as well as sugar because that much sugar would make the food cloying and syrupy. This conditions children to crave unnaturally sweet food, making it difficult to interest them in anything healthier and less sweet.

Why No Hydrogenated Fat?

There are four factors relating to our consumption of fat that influence its effects on us. They are: quantity, saturated or unsaturated, hydrogenation, and free radical damage.

It is best to keep the total amount of fat you eat low — to no more than 30 per cent of your total calorie intake and, ideally, no more than 10 per cent. However, some consumption of fat is essential to good health. The monounsaturates in olive oil and avocados, and polyunsaturates in corn, soya bean and linseed oil provide essential fatty acids that are necessary for the body to function properly. However, most people eat too many *saturated* fats. These are the fats linked to heart disease, found in animal fat, butter and cheese, and in vegetable fats, such as palm kernel oil and coconut oil. It is better to use fats that do positive good, such as extra-virgin olive oil and cold-pressed corn and sunflower oil. Where butter is required for taste, use it, or a margarine that is non-hydrogenated. Why?

Hydrogenation has been in use since the end of the nineteenth century and is a way of making vegetable oil harden at room temperature. Small particles of nickel or copper are added and the mix is heated to very high temperatures under pressure for up to eight hours while hydrogen gas is injected. This process destroys the essential fatty acids in the oil and replaces them with deformed *trans* fatty acids. Although trans fats are found in animal fats, those formed by hydrogenation are misshapen and, as a result, the human body is not well-equipped to deal with them. They also compete with essential fatty acids for absorption in the body. This blocks or delays the work of the essential fatty acids, creating deficiencies and imbalance throughout the metabolism, including fatty deposition in the arteries and liver. A May 1993 study by Rodney Leonard of the Community Nutrition Institute in Washington D.C., has shown that people regularly eating hydrogenated fat weigh at least 2 kg/4½ lb more than those who eat it infrequently, despite consuming the same amount of calories and doing the same amount of exercise. The unnatural trans fats in hydrogenated margarine, in fact, are now recognized to be even more detrimental to health than the saturated fats in butter.

This research, linking hydrogenated fat with heart disease, was published in *The New England Journal of Medicine* in August 1990, but manufacturers have chosen to ignore the evidence and continue to use it in many products, including some so-called health foods. In March 1993, *The Lancet* published the results of an eighteen-year study at the Harvard Medical School involving 85000 American nurses which showed significant increases in coronary heart disease for those consuming hydrogenated fat.

Hydrogenated fat is not always called this in ingredient lists. It can be given as vegetable fat, vegetable margarine or vegetable shortening, hardened vegetable oil, partially hydrogenated fat and mono- and di-glycerides of vegetable oil, even polyunsaturated margarine. Besides being rife in typical supermarket foods, most soya yogurts and soya ice-creams have mono- and di-glycerides in them. Be sure to check the labels.

There are only four brands of non-hydrogenated margarine: Vitaquell, Granose, Granovita and SuperSpread. The first three use saturated fat to harden them. SuperSpread has very little saturated fat and is made from soya protein. It is an emulsion of fine droplets of vegetable oil held together by natural vegetable gums dissolved in water. This is the reverse of butter and margarines, where the droplets of water are separated by a continuous layer of saturated or hydrogenated fat. This means that only half the amount of salt is added to get the same salted taste because it is on the outside of the oil droplets, whereas in butter and margarine, the salt is surrounded by fat. It also spreads more easily, whether at room temperature or straight from the fridge, so less is needed, making it a way of further reducing fat in the diet.

Palm oil contains saturated fat, but it does not raise the overall cholesterol levels. In fact, it increases HDL (good) cholesterol levels. Whole Earth adds a little palm oil to its peanut butter, which keeps the oil from separating and forming a layer on top. If this was not done, the peanut butter would go rancid, lose its fresh-roasted taste, and develop free radicals, which are associated with ageing and degenerative disease.

Processed, refined oils are heated and stripped of their vitamins C and E, which protect against free radicals. When these oils are consumed, they take the place of healthy fatty acids and interfere with cell membrane functions. Frying food also produces free radicals. Use unrefined and extra-virgin oils where possible and fry only as a special treat.

Also, light passing through bottles in which oil is stored produces rancidity and free radicals. It is best to store oil in coloured or opaque bottles in a cupboard and buy it from a shop that shelters it from sunlight.

Free radical damage to the body comes from a variety of sources: pollution, car exhausts, additives, pesticides and de-natured food. However, eating an organic, wholefood diet with plenty of natural vitamins and minerals does help the immune system to balance the effects of free radicals.

Why Organic?

Over 25000 tons of pesticides, herbicides and fungicides are used in Britain every year. More than half of these are known to cause cancer, birth defects, genetic changes or serious irritation if ingested directly, but somehow, we have allowed ourselves to be convinced that food can be exposed to such poisons without absorbing them. This has been proven to be wrong. In 1993, government figures showed detectable residues in a wide range of foods, including 29 per cent of fruit and vegetables, 32 per cent of all cereals, 55 per cent of milk and 48 per cent of potatoes. Buying organic food is the best way to encourage farmers to farm organically and stop the spread of poison in the land, cold water supply and our food.

The term 'organic' is protected by EC law. It means that the product has been rigorously inspected from the farm to the shop by the Soil Association in the UK or by an equivalent organization abroad. Fruit and vegetables have to arrive in a closed case with a certification seal. To be called 'organic', a manufactured food product must contain 95 per cent organic ingredients. If 50–95 per cent are organic, this can be mentioned on the label next to the ingredients.

Organic food may seem to cost more in the short term. However, the long-term cost of *non*-organic agriculture, both to ourselves and the environment, is incalculable. Apart from leaving chemical residues in the water and land and poisoning wildlife, conventional farming uses more crude oil that any other industry in the manufacturing of synthetic fertilizers and pesticides. Millions of tons of topsoil are washed into the sea because soil structure is broken down by chemical fertilizers. Meanwhile, mountains of surplus food are created that are never used or are dumped in Third World countries, putting small farmers there out of business.

Although organic food is more widely available now than ever before, it is still necessary to encourage your local shop or supermarket to stock organic food by buying regularly. Few health food shops will make money out of supplying organic fruit and vegetables, so owners who do are showing a commitment to supplying organic food that is coming out of their pockets. Because organic vegetables are not treated with chemicals after harvesting to keep them looking good, people complain that organic vegetables do not look fresh. There also may only be one delivery a week that is not refrigerated. The best thing is to find out what days the vegetables are delivered and shop that day. The choice and regular availability of a wide range of produce is improving as the market grows. Potatoes, carrots and onions are a fairly cheap and good way to test how much better organic food tastes. More than that, a fresh vegetable, grown as nature intended it, produces a depth and quality of flavour that is all too easily extinguished by factory farming. A friend commented: 'If vegans don't eat animal products for reasons of cruelty, surely they only eat organic vegetables' — certainly food for thought.

Why Vegan?

Whole Earth's roots in macrobiotics meant using little or no dairy and egg products or meat. These days, the questionable quality of the battery-produced egg and factory-farmed meat is further reason to avoid them, even if you are not a confirmed vegan or vegetarian.

More than half of all milk shows pesticide residues and it is difficult to get organic milk. Many people find, too, that they are allergic to cows' milk. Listeria in cheese makes it unwise for pregnant women and those with low immunity to eat soft cheese. There is also the moral issue of keeping a cow lactating its entire life, treating its swollen udders as a milk machine.

General meat production uses added hormones, antibiotics and tranquillizers before leading animals to mass slaughter. However, organic farmers have high welfare standards that will avoid additives and cruelty.

Meat is not necessary for a healthy diet and its production is an inefficient use of agricultural land. Meat production requires six times more land than that needed for a vegan diet to produce the same amount of nutrition. A diet high in whole grains, with a wide variety of vegetables, fruits and pulses, will provide all the nutrients for good health.

How to Read a Label

By law, ingredients in packaged food have to be listed in order of weight, so, if sugar is at the top of the list, there is more sugar than anything else.

Industrially processed food can be a minefield for the unwary. If you're lucky, or buy from manufacturers who value your health, there may be some real food in the packet. There may also be the following:

- *modified starches* these are used to fill out food and give it bulk
- *hydrogenated fats* indigestible fats that also go under the names of vegetable fat or vegetable shortening, mono- and di-glycerides (E471-E472), hardened vegetable oil and partially hydrogenated fat.
- *sugars* other names for them include dextrose, sucrose, glucose, lactose, fructose, invert sugar, refiners' syrup, glucose syrup, as well as Sorbitol, Mannitol and Xylitol
- *artificial sweeteners* aspartame, saccharine
- *hydrolysed vegetable protein* a mixture of amino acids, including dicarboxylic, which affects bodies' growth, and MSG (monosodium glutamate); studies have shown that it causes brain damage in animals and Heinz has ceased its use in its baby foods
- *E numbers* many people are suspicious of anything with an E number attached, so manufacturers have started to list additives by name, the following have been shown to carry risks:

– *colourings* coal tar or azo dyes, cochineal and caramel

– *preservatives* benzoates, sulphates/sulphites, nitrates/nitrites

– *antioxidants* gallates, BHA and BHT

– *emulsifiers and thickeners* calcium disodium, EDTA, carrageenan, tragacanth gum, karaya gum, stearates and polysorbates, di-, tri- and polyphosphates

– *flavour enhancers* glutamates, such as MSG, hydrolysed vegetable protein.

There are dangerous methods of processing food that may not appear on the label.

- *irradiation* By law, if a product has been irradiated, this should be declared on the label. However, if this has been done to an ingredient that makes up less than 25 per cent of a product, it does not have to be declared. So, spices and herbs, which are commonly irradiated, may be an ingredient and the label will not tell you that they have been irradiated.

Irradiated food can deteriorate without showing signs. Greening potatoes, for instance, do not look green after irradiation, but still contain the poison that greens them. This substance causes headaches, nausea and damage to the intestinal tract. Food can be kept longer, but nutrients are lost and bacteria can multiply without providing any characteristic 'off' smell. Irradiation also produces free radicals, which are linked to cancer and damage of the immune system.

The long-term effects of irradiation are not known as it is a relatively new process, but most people would prefer to avoid irradiated food. Hopefully, the consumer will not be duped.

- *genetic engineering* Using cloning techniques, tomatoes have been redesigned to not go soft as they ripen and have Arctic fish genes added to make them more frost-resistant. Yeast has been created that multiplies more quickly. No one knows the long-term unforeseen effects such interference with nature will have. Can genetically altered vegetables get out into nature and multiply wildly? A resistance to viruses from an engineered plant could transfer to its wild counterpart, which could become an uncontainable weed. Could fast-multiplying yeast encourage candida? Equally, most cheese is made with artificial rennet. Some, including all organic cheese, uses a rennet made from wheat. However, most others use a genetically modified enzyme. Is it wise to eat enzymes (which are the building blocks of our own metabolism) created in a laboratory?

- *microwave cooking* This alters the chemical structure of food in a different way to conventional cooking methods. The molecular structure of amino acids is changed and, possibly, also that of carbohydrates. The effects of this on human beings have not been studied.

- *salt* Too much salt in the diet can be unhealthy. Nevertheless, some is necessary. Using sea salt provides trace minerals, such as magnesium and calcium, and reduces the proportion of sodium to around 70 per cent of that in common salt.

Some Notes on Ingredients and Measures

Ingredients

Naturally, these recipes have been tested with Whole Earth products. It is possible to substitute similar items but the results may not be the same. Potential problems could arise with brown rice syrup: Whole Earth's has a much milder flavour than any other brand, similar to that of honey. Also their maize syrup is milder with a less malty flavour than the other malts available.

Less pronounced, but noticeable differences may occur with other ingredients, too. For example, Whole Earth's peanut butter has more of a fresh-roasted flavour than those without added palm oil. The palm oil prevents the peanut oil separating and going rancid, which can make other peanut butter taste muddy. Most of the recipes were tested with original smooth or crunchy peanut butter (with salt). Their American-style peanut butter is slightly sweetened with apple juice and has a smoother, fluffier texture than the original, so it is mentioned by name when important for a recipe. Also, Whole Earth's peanut butters are well-salted, which means that salt may have to be added to a recipe if you use unsalted peanut butter, unless called for or adjusted if other brands are used.

Because of its patented recipe, SuperSpread performs differently to butter or non-hydrogenated margarine. In general, it can be used in any baked recipe that calls for oil, but the amount of liquid should be decreased. It does not fry or melt, but can be stirred or whipped into ingredients. It also substitutes well for mayonnaise and egg-based sauces (see the recipes for Picnic Potato Salad, Runner Beans in Mild Mustard Sauce and Broccoli with SuperSpread Mayonnaise).

Soya milks can vary in taste. All the recipes have been tested with Provamel organic, no-added-sugar soya milk, which is widely available and has a neutral taste.

Soy sauce used should be naturally brewed and fermented. Many types are available and they vary in strength, so you may need to adjust the quantity you use as you cook. The best soy sauces come from health food or oriental shops. Avoid any with sugar in them or a 'non-brewed condiment', which is a mix of artificial colour and chemicals. Shoyu is a Japanese equivalent of soy sauce and tamari is more robust and usually gluten-free.

Carob flour can range from light brown to darkest coffee in colour. The light brown ones do not always have a strong flavour and so more may be needed, while the very dark ones have a burned bitter taste and smell and should be avoided. Try to find a mid-roasted flour for the best results.

Measures

All teaspoons and tablespoons are exact metric equivalents — 5 ml and 15 ml respectively — instead of the slightly larger imperial amounts. This is because most measuring spoons are only available in these sizes nowadays. If you are using an older set of measuring spoons, fill them to below the brim for the same results.

How to Make Soya Yogurt

There is one brand of no-added-sugar plain soya yogurt called Sojasun that is imported from France. It is smooth, milder and naturally sweeter than milk yogurts. Other brands of soya yogurt contain mono- and di-glycerides, a form of indigestible hydrogenated fat. Making your own yogurt as two major advantages. It is possible to use organic soya milk and it is more economical.

Equipment

Food thermometer or specialized yogurt thermometer.
Something to keep the yoghurt warm. A wide-mouthed vacuum flask is best, or a sealed container surrounded by a blanket and kept in a warm place. A yogurt-making machine will also serve this purpose.

Ingredients

Yogurt starter: 2 tbsp fresh, soya or cows' milk yogurt that clearly says 'live' on the label (some health-food shops stock yogurt culture; just use the amount suggested by the manufacturer)
1l/1¾ pints/4 cups soya milk (or less if container is a little smaller)

Method

It is important that all utensils are clean and any residue of soap has been rinsed off (soap residue kills the culture). Boil some water and allow to cool a bit, then pour it into the flask or container (this warms it up so that the yogurt thickens more quickly and removes the risk of it losing heat to a cold container). Empty the flask or container and place the yogurt starter in the bottom.

Heat the soya milk to boiling, then remove it from heat. Place the thermometer in the milk and let it cool to 43–49°C/110–120°F (this takes about 15 minutes, depending on the warmth of the room).

Before the temperature goes any lower, pour some of the milk into the flask or container, with a clean, rinsed spoon, and mix it well with the starter. Stir in the rest of the milk and cover. Check to see if a smooth curd has formed after 4 hours, but it can take up to 16 hours before it is ready, depending on conditions. Otherwise, make it in the evening and check in the morning.

Pour the yogurt into a clean container and leave it to set in the fridge for a couple of hours. When it has a thickish, creamy consistency, take out 2 tbsp of the yogurt to use as the starter for your next batch and put it into a clean jar. This starter should be used between 3 and 10 days later. It can also be frozen to keep it fresh as the culture comes alive again after being defrosted for 15–20 minutes; you can even encourage this by adding some warmed milk and breaking it up.

VARIATION: COWS' MILK YOGURT

This method can also be used to make yogurt from cows' milk. However, it must be boiled, then simmered over a very low heat for 15 minutes to make a thick yogurt. The result will be a yogurt that is milder than most equivalent commercial types, especially after several batches.

STARTERS

Chestnut and Pine Nut Pâté

Why use Real Lemonade in this pâté? Because it blends and brings out the flavour of sweet chestnuts and pine nuts like nothing else. It really is the secret ingredient to this robust, almost meaty, first course.

SERVES 6–8

1½ tbsp vegetable oil
75 g/3 oz/7 tbsp pine nuts
1 medium onion, finely chopped
4 cloves garlic
120 g/4 oz/2 cups fresh, wholemeal breadcrumbs
1 × 435 g/15½ oz/tin *or* 2 cups unsweetened chestnut purée
1 tsp yeast extract *or* dark miso
1 tbsp Kensington Sauce *or* vegan Worcestershire Sauce
4 tbsp Real Lemonade (¼ of a 250-ml/8-fl oz bottle)
sea salt and freshly ground black pepper

Pre-heat the oven to 180°C/350°F/Gas Mark 4

Heat 1 teaspoon of the oil in a frying pan and sauté the pine nuts gently until golden brown, then remove them to drain on kitchen paper. Then fry the onion in the remaining oil for 3 minutes. Crush the garlic and add it to the pan. Sauté until the onion has softened.

In a large bowl, mix the breadcrumbs with the chestnut purée (this is most easily done with your hands or in a food processor). Now add the yeast extract or miso, Kensington or Worcestershire Sauce, Real Lemonade and all but 1 tablespoon of the pine nuts. Stir well and season with plenty of salt and pepper.

Oil a small, non-metallic ovenproof dish well, smooth in the pâté, cover with the reserved pine nuts and bake in the pre-heated oven for 35–45 minutes. Cool in the dish, then serve, sliced, with mild-flavoured toast, rice cakes or on its own with a small salad.

Onion-Smothered Smooth Pâté with Sesame Seeds

Quick, easy and ready to eat within an hour, this mild pâté, spread on toast and topped with sesame-seed-coated onions, is full of contrasting flavours. The red pepper flakes turn up at intervals and add an extra dimension, but can be left out. The pâté can be made several days in advance, but fry the onions on the day of serving.

SERVES 4–6

1 large onion
1½ tsp vegetable oil
300 ml/10 fl oz/1⅛ cups water
1 tsp arrowroot
2 tsp agar agar flakes *or* scant ½ tsp agar agar powder
1 tbsp shoyu *or* soy sauce
2 cloves garlic, crushed
1 tsp garam masala
2 tbsp balsamic vinegar (less if it is not sweet and mild)
½ tsp red pepper flakes (optional)
150 g/5 oz/½ cup smooth (*or* crunchy if serving immediately) original *or* American Style peanut butter
2 tbsp sesame seeds
rye *or* sourdough toast, to serve

Slice the onion and separate into rings. Heat the oil in a medium-sized saucepan or frying pan and sauté the onion rings until soft and browned on the edges. Drain on kitchen paper.

Remove the pan from the heat and wipe out any excess oil. Add the water and arrowroot and stir well to dissolve. Stir in the agar agar. Return to the heat and stir until boiling. Reduce the heat and simmer until the agar agar is dissolved and the liquid has thickened (about 1–2 minutes). Leave to cool for a few minutes.

Add the shoyu or soy sauce, garlic, garam masala, half the balsamic vinegar and the red pepper flakes if using, and mix. Then stir in the peanut butter until smooth. Pour the mixture into a deep soup bowl or small pudding basin. Leave to cool, then chill for 30 minutes, or until set.

Meanwhile, wash the sesame seeds (if they are unhulled) in several changes of water to remove any grit. Drain them, then put them in a pan under the grill on a low heat or in a dry frying pan and heat gently until slowly dried and roasted. Watch carefully — as they burn quite easily — stirring occasionally. Leave to cool.

Just before serving turn the pâté out by sliding a knife around the edges of the pâté, placing a plate over the bowl and turning it over. Toss the onions in the sesame seeds and pile them on top of the pâté. Sprinkle with the remaining balsamic vinegar and serve with warm rye or sourdough toast.

This pâté freezes quite well, although some liquid is lost in the process.

Long-Simmered Mushrooms

This is a wholefood adaptation of one of my mother's favourite starters. She serves four or five mushrooms with cocktail sticks in little Chinese bowls so that guests can sip the steamy, rich broth as well as enjoy the mushrooms. It is worth begging your local health food shop to stock Kensington Sauce, as it is the linchpin of this recipe.

Serves 6–12

550 g–1.25 kg/1¼–2½ lb fresh mushrooms, wiped and left whole, unless very large
120 ml/4 fl oz/½ cup shoyu *or* other soy sauce without sugar
600 ml/1 pint/2⅓ cups water
3 tbsp Kensington Sauce, measured carefully
1 tbsp non-hydrogenated margarine *or* butter
1 tsp dill seeds
large pinch of freshly ground black pepper
3 cloves garlic, peeled and crushed, *or* 1½ tsp garlic powder

Put all the ingredients into a large saucepan. If all the mushrooms do not fit at the beginning, add them in batches as the first ones cook down. Cover and bring to a slow boil, then reduce the heat and simmer for 1–1½ hours, until the broth has penetrated to the centres of the mushrooms. Leave to cool and store in the fridge until needed — up to 3 days. This dish also freezes well.

Reheat to serve.

Hot Peanut Butter Scones with Onion Salad

A mild, marinated, raw onion salad accompanies peanut butter scones fresh from the frying pan and spread with rosemary butter. For convenience, the onion salad can be made up to three to four hours before eating.

MAKES 8

For the Onion Salad
1 large mild *or* red onion, peeled
1 tbsp sea salt

For the dressing
½ tsp mild vinegar (such as balsamic *or* brown rice)
1 tbsp fresh lemon juice
freshly ground black pepper
1½ tbsp olive oil
1 tbsp chopped fresh parsley

For the scones
200 g/7 oz/1½ cups wholemeal flour
½ tsp bicarbonate of soda
½ tsp cream of tartar
½ tsp sea salt (more if using lightly or unsalted peanut butter)
110 g/4 oz/½ cup smooth peanut butter
120 ml/4 fl oz/½ cup soya *or* cows' milk (approximately)
oil, for frying
crushed dried rosemary *or* savory beaten into butter *or* non-hydrogenated margarine *or* SuperSpread to taste, to serve

First, make the Onion Salad by cutting the peeled onion in half from top to bottom. Turn it and slice each half into thin crescents.

Put the onion into a large sieve and sprinkle with the salt. Press until the salt is dissolved, then rinse thoroughly under cold, running water. This makes the onion milder. Drain and dry well on kitchen paper. Mix the dressing ingredients together well in a screw-top jar, pour over the salad and toss until all the onion is coated.

Just before serving, make the scones. Sift the dry ingredients into a medium-sized bowl. Rub in the peanut butter, then gradually add the milk to make a spongy dough — all of the milk may not be needed (this step can be done very quickly in a food processor).

Turn the dough out on to a floured board and roll it out to less than 1 cm/½ in thick. Cut out 8 rounds with a small, round biscuit cutter or drinking glass.

Heat some oil on a griddle or in a heavy based frying pan. Cook the scones over a medium heat, steadily, until they have risen and are brown, then turn them over and cook the other side. Serve hot, spread with the rosemary or savory butter or margarine and the Onion Salad.

Variation
Serve the scones with plain butter, SuperSpread or non-hydrogenated margarine and apricot, blueberry or Hedgerow pure fruit spread, but use half the amount of peanut butter and twice as much milk. This makes a milder peanut butter scone, which tastes better with the fruit spreads.

Papaya with Parsnip Rémoulade

The exquisite pearly orange colour and taste of papaya fruit is joined here with the sweet, nutty taste of grated parsnips and topped with toasted cashews. The classic rémoulade sauce would be made with mayonnaise and mustard, but this lighter version, made with yogurt, complements the papaya and parsnip without overpowering their delicate flavours. If possible, start the parsnip salad a day in advance for extra flavour.

SERVES 4

For the dressing
**120 ml/4 fl oz/½ cup soya *or* cows' milk yogurt
2 tsp mild, organic mustard
1–2 tsp apple juice concentrate**

For the salad
**4 small *or* 2 medium young parsnips
2 ripe papayas, as yellow-skinned as possible
4 tsp unsalted cashews, toasted**

First, mix the dressing ingredients together in a medium-sized bowl, using the larger amount of apple juice concentrate with an acidic cows' milk yogurt, the lesser amount with commercially made soya yogurt.

Wash, peel, then grate the parsnips, making the strips as long as possible. Coat them immediately with the dressing in the bowl to avoid the parsnip discolouring. Keep this overnight or up to 2 days in the fridge for the flavours to develop.

Just before serving, peel the papayas, then slice them in half and scrape out the seeds. Mound some of the parsnip rémoulade in the centre and scatter the toasted cashews on top.

Grapefruit Starters

Here are three cheery ways to eat grapefruit. Two are warmed, while the third is served cold with a berry sauce.

SERVES 4

Grilled Grapefruit with Marmalade (or Pineapple) and Rosemary

2 grapefruit
1 × 140-g/5-oz jar *or* ½ cup/no-added-sugar marmalade *or* pineapple pure fruit spread
2 tsp dried rosemary

Peel the grapefruit, removing all the pith, then slice. Alternatively, slice the grapefruit whole.

Lay the slices in the bottom of the grill pan, removing its rack.

Spread 1 tablespoon of the marmalade or pineapple spread over each slice. Sprinkle the rosemary on top.

Grill under a medium heat for 2–3 minutes until the jam is bubbly and the rosemary crispy. Alternatively, bake the grapefruit slices in the oven, heated to 180°C/350°F/Gas Mark 4, for 5 minutes.

Grilled Grapefruit Halves with Cherries

2 grapefruit, halved
140 g/5 oz cherry pure fruit spread

Loosen the segments of the 4 grapefruit halves, then grill for 5 minutes, until the flesh is warmed through and coloured at the edges. Spread generously with the cherry spread and grill until it is slightly more liquid.

Fresh Grapefruit with Blackcurrant or Hedgerow Sauce

2 grapefruit, halved
140 g/5 oz blackcurrant *or* Hedgerow pure fruit spread

Loosen the segments in each half and remove every other one. Melt the blackcurrant or Hedgerow spread and spoon it into the empty segments. Leave to cool for 10 minutes, then serve.

Leeks in Marmalade Sauce

Fruity olive oil flavours marmalade to make a creamy, peppery sauce for sliced leeks. This makes an excellent starter or side dish.

SERVES 1

1 medium leek
85 ml/3 fl oz/⅓ cup water
1½ tbsp no-added-sugar marmalade
1 tbsp soya milk
1 tbsp olive oil

SERVES 4

4 medium leeks
325 ml/11 fl oz/1⅓ cups water
6 tbsp no-added-sugar marmalade
4 tbsp soya milk
scant 3 tbsp olive oil
freshly ground black pepper

Trim and wash the leeks, remove any hidden grit by slitting them along their length. Slice in 5-mm/¼-in thick rounds. Bring the water to the boil, add the leeks and simmer, covered, until just tender (about 3–4 minutes). Nearly all the water should have evaporated.

Add the marmalade, soya milk and olive oil and stir until heated through. Serve warm, seasoned with black pepper.

Cold Sesame Noodles

Visitors to Chinese restaurants in New York rave about this starter, which often arrives as guests are perusing the menu. Soft noodles are dressed in a rich sesame and peanut sauce that can range from piquant to fiery hot. This version comes from Annie and Jennifer Weisberg. The best-textured wholegrain noodles available are the organic Italian brands of wholewheat noodles or Japanese buckwheat noodles (soba). They are both nearly as soft as white noodles when cooked. This dish can be made in advance and chilled.

Serves 4

225 g/8 oz wholemeal *or* buckwheat noodles
2 tbsp toasted sesame oil

For the sauce
2 medium cloves garlic
120 g/4 oz/⅜ cup light tahini
½ jar/165 g/25½ oz/½ heaped cup smooth peanut butter
120 ml/4 fl oz/½ cup steeped black tea
2½ tbsp soy sauce
chilli oil to taste: mild, a few drops; up to 2 tbsp for very hot
1 tbsp apple juice concentrate *or* brown rice syrup
1 tbsp red wine vinegar

For topping
snipped green tops of 5 spring onions
½ cucumber, cut into julienne

Cook the noodles according to the directions on the packet. Drain and rinse in cold water. Toss with half of the sesame oil.

The sauce can be made in a bowl or in a food processor. Crush the garlic and mix in the tahini, peanut butter, tea, soy sauce, chilli oil, apple juice concentrate or brown rice syrup, vinegar, and remaining toasted sesame oil.

Put the noodles into a large bowl and pour over the sauce. Stir well, (the noodles should be wet, but slightly sticky). Note that if only a small amount of chilli oil is used, it will be necessary to add a little vegetable oil to thin the sauce. Serve cold with the spring onion and cucumber in separate bowls, so guests can help themselves to the toppings.

California Sushi Nori Rolls

Although not traditional, using tinned rice means that this is practically an instant meal. A really hungry person could eat all three rolls as a main course, but, served as a starter, this amount should serve three people. You can use any filling that you fancy, but the following two California-style combinations are delicious.

SERVES 1–3

1 × 440-g/15½-oz tin *or* 3 cups Organic Ready Rice
2½ tsp mirin (optional)
2 tsp brown rice vinegar
1 tsp shoyu *or* soy sauce
1 tsp apple juice concentrate
1 tsp wasabi (Japanese green horseradish) powder
3 sheets nori seaweed

Cucumber, pepper and avocado filling
¼ cucumber, cut into julienne
½ yellow pepper, cut into julienne
1 small avocado, cut into thick strips, with a little brown rice vinegar sprinkled over

Asparagus filling
asparagus tips, steamed with a little made-up wasabi dotted over

Other fillings
cooked, sliced, fresh *or* dried mushrooms; toasted sesame seeds; blanched spinach; French beans *or* blanched strips of carrot

Steam the Organic Ready Rice, forking through it lightly to disperse any lumps.

In a medium-sized bowl, mix together the mirin, if using, brown rice vinegar, shoyu or soy sauce and apple juice concentrate. Add the steamed brown rice and stir lightly. On a small plate, make up the wasabi by adding a few drops of water and mixing until slightly liquid.

If the nori is dark green, it will need to be toasted. Do this by waving it over a hot burner for a few seconds until it turns a lighter green and crisps up a bit. It burns easily so watch it carefully.

Lay a sheet of nori on a flat surface or large plate. Mound a third of the rice mixture along the edge closest to you. Place your choice of filling along the middle. Roll up the sheet from the edge nearest you, packing it firmly, until you have a long, thin roll (use a bamboo rolling mat to do this if you have one). To seal the roll, dip your finger in the wasabi or plain water and draw a line along the edge of the nori sheet. Lay the roll so that the seam is underneath. Cut each roll into 4 pieces, using a very sharp knife.

Gingered Peanut Soufflés

Here are moist little soufflés made without eggs. They are flavoured with fresh ginger and cumin and make an unusual first course.

Makes 4

non-hydrogenated margarine, for greasing
110 g/4 oz/½ cup smooth peanut butter
250 ml/8 fl oz/1 cup soya milk
2 tbsp wholemeal flour
2 tsp soy sauce
1 tsp arrowroot
1 large clove garlic, crushed
1 tbsp fresh, grated ginger, or more to taste
1 tsp ground cinnamon
1 tsp ground cumin
1 tsp baking powder
¼ tsp bicarbonate of soda

Pre-heat the oven to 190°C/375°F/Gas Mark 5 and generously grease 4 individual ramekins with non-hydrogenated margarine

In a medium-sized bowl, whisk the peanut butter, soya milk and flour together until you have a smooth, creamy, mixture.

Add the rest of the ingredients, except the baking powder and bicarbonate of soda and mix well. Taste and add a little more ginger if you prefer.

Add the baking powder and bicarbonate of soda and mix very well. Immediately, pour the mixture into the prepared ramekins, put into the pre-heated oven and try not to open it for 25 minutes. By then, the soufflés should be puffy and browned on the top. Serve immediately, if possible, as they will collapse, just like 'real' soufflés.

Tart Peanut Dip for Crudités

This tangy dip has a very modern flavour. The tart lemon sets off the shoyu and peanut paste and the parsley links them together. The quality and freshly roasted taste of the peanut butter makes all the difference to this dish.

SERVES 3–4
60 g/2 oz/¼ cup smooth peanut butter
25 g/1 oz/¼ cup onion, finely chopped
50 ml/2 fl oz/¼ cup fresh lemon juice
1 tbsp shoyu *or* soy sauce
2 large cloves garlic, crushed
15 g/½ oz/¼ cup fresh parsley, finely chopped

In a bowl or food processor, mix all the ingredients together. Serve at room temperature. This dip is delicious with tomatoes, spring onions and other crudités.

Creamy Peanut Onion Dip

This is a delicious dip, strongly flavoured with asafoetida or caraway. Make it with any of the peanut butters, although Whole Earth American Style will make it sweeter, as will soya yogurt. When chilled, it thickens, making a great sandwich spread. Try the other dips to ring the changes.

SERVES 4
6 tbsp peanut butter, smooth *or* crunchy
120 ml/4 fl oz/½ cup soya *or* cows' milk yogurt
1 tsp dried onion powder *or* chopped onion and chives
½ tsp asafoetida *or* 1 tsp caraway seeds
crisps *or* crackers, to serve

Mix the ingredients together well. Serve with crisps or crackers.

Variation: Onion Dip
**250 ml/8 fl oz/1 cup soya *or* cows' milk yogurt
4 tbsp mayonnaise *or* tofu mayonnaise
4–6 tbsp soy sauce, to taste
8 tbsp Kensington Sauce
4 tsp onion powder**

Mix the ingredients together well.

Other quick dips
**120 ml/4 fl oz/½ cup soya yogurt
120 ml/4 fl oz/½ cup Reduced Calorie Thousand Island Dressing
4 tsp dried mint**

Mix the ingredients together well.

**120 ml/4 fl oz/½ cup Lemon and Garlic Dressing
4 tbsp soya yogurt
4 tsp dried dill weed**

Mix the ingredients together well.

**185-g/6½-oz block of firm tofu, liquidized
120 ml/4 fl oz/½ cup Oil Free vinaigrette
4 tsp dried tarragon
120 ml/4 fl oz/½ cup soya yogurt**

Mix the ingredients together well.

**1 × 440-g/15½-oz tin no-added-sugar baked beans
up to 250 ml/8 fl oz/1 cup soya *or* other yogurt
up to ½ tsp celery seeds**

Whizz three-quarters of the contents of the tin of baked beans with their liquid in a food processor or liquidizer. Add the yogurt slowly until it is the desired consistency (yogurt varies in thickness). Mix in the celery seeds and remaining beans.

**250 ml/8 fl oz/1 cup soya *or* other yogurt
110 g/4 oz/½ cup Savoury Nut Butter
onion powder to taste**

Particularly good with fresh celery or rice cakes.

HOT SOUPS

Warm Apricot Soup with Walnuts

This clear, fruit soup makes a delicate starter for a dinner party or a wonderful breakfast. The allspice gives it a completely different character, but try it first adorned only with fresh walnuts. Try using the organic apricot pure fruit spread in this recipe as it has a really special taste.

Serves 4 in large bowls, 8 in Japanese soup bowls

2 × 283-g/10-oz jars apricot pure fruit spread
1 tsp ground allspice (optional)
750 ml/1¼ pints/3 cups/3 jars water
25–50 g/1–2 oz/4–8 tbsp very fresh walnut pieces

Warm 4 soup bowls, or 8 small, Japanese soup bowls.

Put the apricot spread and the allspice, if using, in a saucepan. Add the water to the pan and heat to boiling point, stirring to break up the apricot spread.

Pour the soup into the bowls and garnish with half the walnuts. These will absorb the liquid quickly, so offer the remaining walnuts to guests to be added to the soup while they are eating.

Hungarian Cherry Soup

This is a clear, cherry-red soup, flavoured with lemon. Serve warm or chilled as a refreshing beginning to a meal.

Serves 3

1 × 283-g/10-oz jar cherry no-added-sugar pure fruit spread
475 ml/16 fl oz/2 cups/2 jars water
1 organic or unwaxed lemon
1 tsp arrowroot
zest of 1 organic orange and/or lime, to garnish (optional)

Empty the cherry spread into a saucepan. Add the water to the pan. Slice the outermost layer of zest from the lemon, including as little pith as possible, then slice it into julienne. Put half the strips into the soup (saving the rest to garnish it later). Bring the soup to the boil, reduce the heat and cook for 5 minutes.

Add 2 tablespoons of lemon juice from the peeled lemon to the pan and cook for a further 5 minutes. Dissolve the arrowroot in a little water and add to the pan, stirring. Cook a further 2 minutes until the soup has thickened slightly.

Pour the soup into 3 small bowls, dividing the whole cherries from the spread between them. Garnish with the reserved lemon strips. Add the orange and lime zest julienne strips, if using, for a colourful garnish. Serve warm or cold.

Almond Soup

Ground almonds, bitter oranges and onions combine to make a rich, thick soup redolent of southern Spain.

Serves 4

2 tbsp olive oil
4 tbsp onion, chopped
100 g/3½ oz/1¼ cups ground almonds
½ tsp chopped fresh ginger
1 large clove garlic, crushed
½ tsp sea salt
400 ml/14 fl oz/1¾ cups water
140 g/5 oz/½ cup/½ jar Orange Shred (sweet 'n' fruity)
4 green olives in brine, sliced, to garnish (optional)

In a heavy based saucepan, heat the olive oil and fry the onion, ground almonds, ginger, garlic and salt over a very low heat. Stir regularly for 5–7 minutes until the onions are soft and the almonds golden brown.

Mix the water and Orange Shred well in a bowl or food processor. Transfer it to the saucepan and heat through. Pour the soup into 4 small bowls and garnish with the green olives, if using.

Spiced Marmalade Soup with Macadamia Nuts

Orange shreds and flecks of black pepper float in this clear, orange broth, which looks pretty served in small Japanese or Chinese soup bowls. Put a bowl of macadamia nuts in the middle of the table for everyone to add to the soup as they like.

Serves 4–5

1 × 283-g/10-oz jar no-added-sugar marmalade
475 ml/16 fl oz/2 cups/2 jars water
4 tsp apple juice concentrate
2 tbsp pickling spice, including a dried chilli tied in a piece of muslin
freshly ground black pepper
1 × 75-g/3-oz packet salted macadamia nuts, to serve

Put the marmalade in a saucepan and add the water. Stir in the apple juice concentrate, add the pickling spice bag and grind in some pepper.

Bring to the boil, then simmer, uncovered, for 10–15 minutes.

Remove the spice bag and pour the soup into 4 or 5 small bowls, dividing the orange shreds equally. Leave it to cool a minute, then float 2 or 3 macadamia nuts on top of each bowl and serve. Serve the remaining macadamia nuts separately.

Roasted Nut Cream Soup with Green Peppercorns

This is a rich, smooth, creamy soup, with crunchy pieces of nuts and green peppercorns. Served in small bowls or cups, this is an unusual wake-up-the-tastebuds starter.

Serves 4

1 × 270-g/9½-oz jar Three Nut Butter
600 ml/1 pint/2½ cups water

**2 tsp arrowroot
4 tbsp shoyu *or* soy sauce
2⅔ tbsp balsamic vinegar
1–1½ tsp freeze-dried green peppercorns, crushed with the back of a spoon**

Empty the Three Nut Butter into a medium-sized saucepan. Add the water to the pan. Whisk the arrowroot with some of the water until it is dissolved and add to the pan.

Add the shoyu or soy sauce, 2 tablespoons of the balsamic vinegar and the green peppercorns and heat until smooth and creamy, stirring occasionally.

Divide the soup between 4 small bowls, and add ½ teaspoon of the remaining balsamic vinegar to each. Stir once with a spoon, to make a swirly, marbled pattern, and serve warm.

Organic Cream of Tomato Soup

This tastes like a superior tinned soup, it is just as quick and there is no added sugar. Soya milk is useful because there is an organic variety and it comes in long life packs. It also becomes nice and thick when it is mixed with a lightly acidic vegetable or fruit.

Serves 1

**300 ml/10 fl oz/1⅛ cups organic soya milk
5 tbsp organic tomato ketchup
3–4 drops Tabasco sauce (optional)**

In a saucepan, mix the milk and tomato ketchup and heat together, gently, until hot (about 1 minute). Do not let it boil. For added kick, add the optional 3–4 drops of Tabasco sauce.

Kensington Soup

This is a well-flavoured, creamy, quick soup that makes a good lunch with some oatcakes. It is also nice chilled.

Serves 4–6

1 × 425-g/15-oz tin/2 cups cooked white beans (such as butter, haricot or cannellini (optional)
250 ml/8 fl oz/1 cup water or bean stock
1 l/1¾ pints/4 cups soya milk
50 ml/2 fl oz/¼ cup Kensington Sauce (measured carefully)
2–4 tbsp soy sauce (depending on its strength)
1 tbsp non-hydrogenated margarine or butter
2 tsp garlic powder
½ tsp dried dill weed or 1 tsp dried savory
4 tbsp pine nuts or oatcakes, to serve

Put the cooked beans, if using, into a large saucepan with the water or stock and heat until boiling. Cook for 5 minutes. Add the remaining ingredients except the pine nuts or oatcakes and heat through. If you are not using beans, then just mix all the ingredients together except the pine nuts or oatcakes, and heat through.

Taste and add more soy sauce if necessary. Serve with the pine nuts on top or with the oatcakes.

Warm Hummus Soup

This is a warming, thick and nourishing soup that is delicious without adding anything else, but roasted cumin seeds give it an added dimension. Note that the Whole Earth Hummus is especially thick, so, if you use any other hummus, use less water.

Serves 2

¼ tsp whole cumin seeds (optional)
1 × 300-g/10½-oz/1¼ cups Hummus
250 ml/8 fl oz/1 cup water

In a small saucepan, dry roast the cumin seeds, if using, over a low heat until they are brown and fragrant. Remove them from the pan.

Put the hummus and water into the saucepan over a low heat and mix, breaking up the lumps to form a smooth soup. Continue to heat through over a low heat. Do not boil.

Pour the soup into 2 bowls, then crush the cumin seeds lightly and sprinkle over the top.

Variation
In place of the cumin, try a pinch of dried thyme on top or a few drops of chilli sauce or some garlic mixed in.

Smooth Potato Soup

Although this has an unlikely sounding combination of ingredients, this soup makes a thick, warming and delicate one-dish meal. Left-over mashed potatoes work well, but it is also worth making the soup from scratch. Only the question of aesthetic attractiveness prevents leaving the skins on the potatoes, so use unpeeled potatoes to save time, and vitamins, if you do not mind.

Serves 4

400 g/14 oz/2 cups mashed potatoes (made from 450 g/1 lb peeled potatoes)
900 ml/1½ pints/3½ cups soya or cows' milk
1 tbsp grated or finely chopped onion
1 tbsp non-hydrogenated margarine or butter or SuperSpread
50 g/2 oz/¼ cup smooth peanut butter or Savoury Nut Butter
4 tbsp organic ketchup
1 tsp garlic powder or 1–2 cloves garlic, crushed
sea salt
cumin seeds, to garnish

In a medium-sized saucepan, put the mashed potatoes, milk, onion, margarine or butter or SuperSpread and peanut butter or Savoury Nut Butter and cook over a medium heat to boiling point. Stir in the ketchup and garlic and cook until warmed through.

Season to taste with salt, pour the soup into 4 bowls and garnish with the cumin seeds. Leave it to cool a little before serving as it will be piping hot.

Tomato and Bean Soup

This is a quick, nourishing, full-bodied soup that would serve two with some crusty rolls for lunch or four as a starter.

SERVES 2–4

1 tbsp oil
1 medium onion *or* the whites of 3 spring onions *or* 1 small leek, chopped
2 cloves garlic, crushed
1 × 440-g/15½-oz tin no-added-sugar Campfire *or* Organic baked beans
4 tbsp no-added-sugar ketchup *or* 200 g/7 oz tinned plum tomatoes
475 ml/16 fl oz/2 cups water *or* stock
½ tsp dried basil

Heat the oil in a medium-sized saucepan and fry the onion or spring onion or leek until limp, then add the garlic and stir.

If a food processor is available, whizz the garlic and onion and half the baked beans with the ketchup or tomatoes. If making by hand, mash half the baked beans well in a bowl and add the garlic and onion and ketchup or tomatoes, mixing them together.

Return the mixture to the pan, add the water or stock, remaining baked beans and the dried basil and heat until just boiling.

Cream of Peanut Soup

This is a thick, creamy soup, flavoured with cardamom and celery. Good for a winter's evening.

SERVES 4

1 medium onion
2 large celery sticks
1 tbsp vegetable oil
2 tbsp arrowroot
3 tbsp water
1 l/1¾ pints/4 cups soya *or* cows' milk
1 bay leaf
½ tsp ground cardamom
225 g/8 oz/1 cup smooth peanut butter
sea salt
½ tsp caraway seeds (optional)

Finely chop the onion and celery. In a heavy based medium-sized saucepan, sauté them in the oil until golden brown.

Dissolve the arrowroot in the water, then add to the saucepan together with the milk. Add the bay leaf and cardamom and slowly bring to the boil, stirring occasionally to prevent the soya milk sticking. Reduce the heat and simmer until the milk begins to thicken. Remove from the heat and whisk in the peanut butter in several batches.

Remove the bay leaf and add salt to taste. Reheat if necessary, then serve in 4 warmed bowls with the caraway seeds, if liked, sprinkled on top.

CHILLED SOUPS

Avocado and Lemonade Soup with Tarragon Ice Flakes

This is a silky smooth, light green summer soup. The tarragon ice cubes melt to flavour it, but your guests will never guess the secret ingredient that delicately perfumes the avocado.

Serves 6

1 tbsp fresh *or* 1 tsp dried tarragon
1 × 740-ml/1¼-pint bottle Real Lemonade *or* 3 × 250-ml/8-fl oz bottles
6 small avocados *or* equivalent, preferably with light green, smooth skin

Make 12 small ice cubes, with a sprig or couple of leaves of tarragon in the centre when you freeze them (or use 6 yogurt pots and make thin ice discs). Allow 2 hours or more, depending on your freezer, for this.

If you can, remove the lid from the lemonade bottle(s) several days in advance and keep it (them) in the fridge so that the bubbles will disappear. Even if you have done this, however, it will still be necessary to whizz the lemonade in a food processor to beat out all the bubbles. When you do this, remove the lid or stopper of the processor to let the carbon dioxide out between whizzes until very little 'head' is left.

Just before serving, peel the avocados and put the flesh into the food processor or liquidizer with the lemonade. Whizz to make the soup. Pour the soup into 6 small bowls, add the ice cubes or flakes to each one and serve.

Golden Soup

Galangal is available dried in supermarkets (in this recipe, ground ginger will not work as a substitute).

SERVES 4

250 ml/8 fl oz/1 cup soya milk (cows' milk does not work as well)
250 ml/8 fl oz/1 cup water
2 tsp dried galangal pieces
1 × 283-g/10-oz jar Golden Plum pure fruit spread

Pour the soya milk and water into a jug and infuse the galangal in it for at least 30 minutes. Chill both the milk mixture and the Golden Plum spread.

Sieve the milk into the goblet of a liquidsizer, or into a food processor, pressing to squeeze the last drops of flavour out of the galangal. Add the Golden Plum and whizz. Pour into small bowls and serve chilled.

Blackcurrant and Lemon Soup

This is a refreshing, slightly tart summer soup with a rich depth of colour.

SERVES 4–5

2 × 283-g/10-oz jars blackcurrant pure fruit spread
1 1/1¾ pints/4 cups/4 jars water
grated zest of half an organic *or* unwaxed lemon
2 tsp fresh lemon juice
lemon wedges, to garnish

Put the blackcurrant spread into a medium-sized saucepan, then add the water. Add the lemon zest and heat to boiling point, stirring to break up the jam. Add the lemon juice.

Switch off the heat and leave the soup to come to room temperature. Pour it into 4–5 small bowls. The soup tastes best just after making and does not benefit from chilling. Serve garnished with the lemon wedges, so guests can add more lemon juice, if desired.

SALADS

Salad of Radicchio and Rocket with Artichokes and Walnuts

This is an elegant first-course salad with a bitter marmalade dressing. Wonderful for a dinner party or lunch, the dressing really complements the mildly astringent leaves supermarkets sell in their speciality sections and which are often available organically grown.

SERVES 4

For the dressing
4 tbsp no-added-sugar marmalade (preferably not chunky cut)
4 tbsp extra-virgin olive oil
3 small cloves garlic, crushed
4 tbsp water
2 tbsp fresh lemon juice
freshly ground black pepper

For the salad
50 g/2 oz rocket, washed and torn
small head radicchio, washed and torn
15 g/½ oz young sorrel leaves, shredded
up to half a head Chinese leaf, shredded
2 small yellow peppers, seeded and roughly chopped
1 × 285-g/10-oz jar antipasto artichoke hearts (Carciofini), drained
100 g/3½ oz/½ cup walnut halves
1 large avocado, peeled, chopped and mixed with a little lemon juice
(optional)

Make the dressing by mixing the marmalade and olive oil together with a fork to a smooth consistency. Add the garlic, water, lemon juice and pepper and mix again.

To make the salad, put the prepared leaves and yellow pepper into a bowl and mix. Add the artichoke hearts, walnuts and avocado, if using, and toss with the dressing. Alternatively, arrange the salad ingredients on 4 plates and drizzle over the dressing.

Green and Yellow Salad with Apricot and Lime Dressing

Slightly sour green olives and a zing of lime act as a contrast to mildly sweet apricot, fennel and yellow pepper in this crunchy, fresh-tasting salad.

Serves 4

1 small fennel bulb, sliced
1 small head of lettuce (any type), torn
1 yellow pepper, sliced
65 g/2½ oz/½ cup stoned green olives in brine
3 celery sticks, sliced

For the dressing
½ tsp grated zest of an organic *or* unwaxed lime
4 tbsp lime juice
4 tbsp apricot pure fruit spread
3 tbsp water
4 tsp walnut *or* vegetable oil
freshly ground black pepper *or* green peppercorns

Prepare the salad in a large bowl.

Mix the dressing ingredients in a screw-top jar and shake well. Just before serving, toss the salad with the dressing.

Sweet-Sour Carrot Salad

A carrot salad to ring the changes. Very fresh carrots have a sweet flavour, while the olives bring a slightly sour contrast and the dressing adds an extra fruitiness. It is all topped with sweet-sour toasted seeds.

Serves 4

6 tbsp sunflower seeds
3 tbsp pumpkin seeds
2⅔ tbsp Reduced Calorie Oil Free Vinaigrette
4 medium very fresh, sweet carrots
6 stoned green olives in brine, drained and chopped

Dry roast the seeds in a frying pan, stirring until golden. Turn off the heat, add 2 teaspoons vinaigrette and stir until the heat evaporates the liquid, leaving an aromatic flavour on the toasted seeds.

Grate the carrots and stir in the remaining vinaigrette. Mix in the chopped green olives.

Just before serving, sprinkle half the toasted seeds over the salad. Serve the remaining seeds separately to add as the salad is eaten.

Lemonade Jelly with Marigolds

Marigolds add a subtle flavour and scent to this mildly sweet jelly, but the real delight is the lemonade tingle trapped in it, surprising you on the first bite. As a novelty salad, it makes a lovely, colourful addition to a summer buffet table. For such occasions just double the recipe and use a medium-sized bowl.

Serves 6

1 × 740-ml/1¼-pint bottle no-added-sugar Real Lemonade
1¼ tsp agar agar powder *or* 1¼ tbsp agar agar flakes
1–4 marigold flowers (*Calendula officinalis*, not tiny Tagetes, which are poisonous)
1 large sprig fresh *or* 1 tsp dried tarragon

Pour half the Real Lemonade into a medium-sized saucepan and stir in the agar agar. Wash the marigolds carefully and toss the least pretty ones into the pan (or, if using only one, remove and reserve most of the petals and put in the head). Bring to the boil and simmer gently for 2–3 minutes or until the agar agar has dissolved. Leave to cool for 5 minutes.

Remove the cooked marigolds. Add the remaining Real Lemonade to the pan and stir well. Pour the jelly into a clear bowl (so the jelly can be seen). Strip the petals from the reserved marigolds (or use the reserved petals from the single one) and sprinkle them and the tarragon leaves over the top, making a floating design. Chill until set (1–2 hours). If you have them, decorate with more fresh marigolds in the centre, before serving.

Walnut and Caper Rice Salad

The combination of very fresh walnuts and capers preserved in vinegar is wonderful. Sun-dried tomatoes and fresh coriander add delicious accents, but could be substituted with other things in the cupboard.

SERVES 2 AS A MAIN COURSE OR 4 IF ONE OF SEVERAL SALADS

1 × 440-g/15½-oz tin or 3 cups Organic Ready Rice *or* cooked brown rice
3–4 tbsp drained cooked kidney *or* white beans
large handful of roughly chopped fresh coriander *or* parsley
6–8 stoned green *or* black olives (optional)
1 tsp capers in vinegar
8 walnut halves, as fresh as possible
4 sun-dried tomatoes soaked in oil, sliced, *or* fresh tomatoes
1 tsp olive oil (can be from the sun-dried tomatoes)
½ tsp balsamic *or* brown rice vinegar *or* lemon juice (optional)

Fork through the rice and mix in the beans. Stir in the remaining ingredients and serve.

Georgian Kidney Beans with Plum Vinaigrette

According to my friend, Ivana, in the Balkans mothers-in-law test daughters-in-law on their cooking skills by the texture of the beans they have cooked. 'I see you added salt to the cooking pot,' means 'You are so hopeless you don't even know salt toughens beans and should be added after they are cooked.'

This recipe, adapted from Darra Goldstein's A Taste of Russia (Robert Hale, 1985 (out of print)) features a sweet-and-sour dressing which truly complements kidney beans. Tinned kidney beans can be used, but they do not have the chance to absorb the flavours during cooking and so are really second best.

SERVES 4

350 g/12 oz/2 cups dried kidney beans

For cooking the beans
2 cloves garlic, halved
½ tsp red pepper flakes *or* crushed fresh red pepper
2 bay leaves
4 tbsp red wine vinegar

For the dressing
2 cloves garlic, crushed
½ tsp red pepper flakes, *or* crushed fresh red pepper
¼ tsp sea salt
freshly ground black pepper
1½ tbsp chopped fresh coriander or more, to taste
4 tbsp red wine vinegar
175 g/6 oz/¾ cup Golden Plum pure fruit spread

Pick over, wash and soak the beans overnight in ample water to cover (or bring to the boil and cover tightly for 1 hour). Drain and add water to cover in a large, heavy based saucepan.

Add the ingredients for cooking the beans. Boil rapidly for 10 minutes, then simmer until tender (45 minutes–1 hour). Drain.

While the beans are still warm, add the ingredients for the dressing. Leave the beans to cool, then chill until you want to use them, but serve them at room temperature.

Cucumber and Onion Salad in Sweet Vinegar

Try this salad together with a group of other fresh salads or with a fried dish. The sliced cucumber and onion are marinated in sweetened vinegar for a refreshing flavour. For a decorative touch, tiny blue borage flowers look very pretty floating in the marinade.

175 ml/6 fl oz/¾ cup white wine vinegar
120 ml/4 fl oz/½ cup water
2 tbsp brown rice syrup
1 medium cucumber, sliced
1 small onion or 2 spring onions, sliced
borage flowers (optional)

Mix the liquid ingredients together in a bowl and add the sliced cucumber, onion and borage flowers, if using. Leave the cucumber and onion to marinate for at least 30 minutes. They are especially delicious after 24 hours, but remove the cucumber and onion from the marinade to a jar after that. The vinegar can then be reused until it becomes cloudy.

Blackcurrant Salad Mould with Chinese Leaf

Salad moulds are useful at a barbecue or large party because they can be made well in advance and add an alternative texture to the rest of the fare there. This one is only mildly sweet and finicky children will not notice the green stuff hidden inside.

SERVES 6–8

1 tsp agar agar powder *or* 1 tbsp agar agar flakes
400 ml/14 fl oz/1¾ cups water
2 × 283-g/10-oz jars blackcurrant pure fruit spread
2 tbsp Reduced Calorie Thousand Island Dressing
120 g/4½ oz/1 cup Chinese leaf, finely chopped if not using a food processor, plus extra to garnish
4 tbsp soya *or* mild cows' milk yogurt, to serve

Rinse a 1.2-litre/2-pint jelly or ring mould with cold water and drain.

Put the agar agar and half the water into a saucepan and heat to boiling point. Reduce the heat and simmer for 1 minute, or until the agar agar has dissolved. Leave it to cool for a few minutes.

While the jelly mixture is cooling, put the blackcurrant spread, the remaining water, half the Thousand Island Dressing and 120 g/4½ oz/1 cup Chinese leaf into a food processor and whizz. Alternatively, just mix the ingredients together well in a bowl.

Add the agar agar water, whizz again then pour the mixture into the mould. Chill the jelly until it has set (1–2 hours).

Unmould the jelly and garnish with the extra shredded Chinese leaf. Mix the yogurt with the remaining Thousand Island Dressing and put into a small serving bowl for people to help themselves to, then serve immediately.

Picnic Potato Salad

SuperSpread makes an excellent mayonnaise dressing that will not spoil in hot temperatures, is lower in calories and is less expensive than tofu mayonnaises.

Serves 4

**450 g/1 lb waxy potatoes
4 tbsp SuperSpread
4 tbsp soya milk
1 tsp mild mustard
1 large clove garlic, crushed
½ tsp dried rosemary *or* tarragon (optional)
1–2 spring onions *or* 2 tbsp finely chopped onion**

Boil the potatoes in their jackets until tender. Drain, then cut them into chunks and leave to cool.

Whisk the SuperSpread, soya milk and mustard together. Stir in the garlic and rosemary or tarragon, if using.

Slice the spring onions finely and add them or the onion to the potatoes. Pour the dressing over and stir. Chill before serving.

Reduced Calorie Parsley Potato Salad

This is a creamy potato salad with a fraction of the calories of mayonnaise.

Serves 4

**900 g/2 lbs potatoes
120 ml/4 fl oz/½ cup Reduced Calorie Lemon and Garlic Dressing
handful of fresh parsley, torn
sea salt and freshly ground black pepper**

Scrub the potatoes and chop them into bite-sized chunks, then steam for about 15 minutes or until they are tender, but not soft. Drain and leave them to cool for a few minutes until they are room temperature. Put them into a bowl.

Pour the Lemon and Garlic Dressing over the potatoes, add the parsley and stir to combine. Add salt and pepper to taste. Chill if not serving immediately.

Curried Apple Salad

This is a useful salad to serve at a barbecue or picnic because the SuperSpread mayonnaise can stand warm temperatures. It is a sort of curried Waldorf salad with toasted almonds and coconut instead of walnuts and was highly popular among tasters for its robust flavours.

Serves 6–8

For the dressing
1 × 250-g/9-oz tub/1 cup SuperSpread
3 tbsp mustard
3 tbsp apple juice concentrate
4 tbsp fresh lime juice
1½ tsp mild curry powder

For the salad
4 medium, slightly tart apples (Coxes or Granny Smiths are good)
2 celery sticks, sliced
25 g/1 oz/¼ heaped cup flaked almonds
25 g/1 oz/¼ heaped cup desiccated coconut

Make the dressing by combining all the dressing ingredients in a medium-sized bowl.

Quarter and core the apples, then slice them thinly. Add them to the dressing, together with the sliced celery and mix. Chill until ready to serve.

Dry roast the flaked almonds in a frying pan, stirring occasionally, until they are golden brown. Remove them from the pan and leave to cool, while dry roasting the coconut, which only takes a few seconds in a hot pan. Scatter both over the salad just before serving.

Motley Bean Salad or Stew

With its creamy, smoky, slightly sweet-and-sour sauce, this salad is adapted from an American 1950s-style 'straight from the store cupboard' recipe from Kat Grossman. It tastes delicious warm as a main course and the quantity this recipe makes is enough to have it warm one evening and the left-overs as a salad the next, but keep it chilled in between and use it all within two days.

Serves 8–10

3 tbsp vegetable oil
2 × 220-g/7½-oz packets smoked tofu
2–3 large onions, sliced
5–6 tbsp organic brown rice syrup, to taste
3 tbsp cider vinegar
1 clove garlic, crushed
1 × 415-g/14-oz tin butter beans without added sugar, drained
1 × 415-g/14-oz tin kidney beans without added sugar, drained
1 × 440-g/15½-oz tin no-added-sugar baked beans
1 × 415-g/14-oz tin flageolet beans, undrained
sea salt and freshly ground black pepper
fresh tomatoes, sliced, to serve

Heat the oil in a very large saucepan, or a large frying pan and then transfer it to a casserole. While the oil is heating, dice the smoked tofu and sauté it lightly. Push the centres of the onion slices to separate the rings, add them to the saucepan or casserole and sauté until cooked through.

Add the brown rice syrup, vinegar and garlic, cover and cook for 5 minutes.

Pour all the beans on to the onions in the saucepan or casserole, and mix. Season with salt and pepper to taste. If using a saucepan, simmer, stirring occasionally, for 20–30 minutes. If using a casserole, bake for half an hour at 180°C/350°F/Gas Mark 4.

Eat the beans warm as a stew or leave them to cool, chill and serve as a salad. Serve with fresh tomato to bring out the flavour of the hot or cold beans. This dish can be frozen, but heat it through well after defrosting and note that the smoked tofu will lose its characteristic texture.

Marinated Mushrooms

They are best after a day in the fridge, but they can be eaten at any time.

SERVES 6

1 tbsp Kensington Sauce
1 tbsp shoyu *or* tamari soy sauce (use the best quality, if possible)
1 tbsp fresh lemon juice
freshly ground black pepper
450 g/1 lb fresh mushrooms, organic if possible
sea salt

In a medium-sized bowl, mix the Kensington Sauce, shoyu or tamari, lemon juice and pepper.

Wipe the mushrooms, slice them and add them to the bowl. Mix them well with the marinade. Chill them for a day, stirring occasionally. Taste and add a little salt, if needed, before serving.

Hummus Cabbage Salad

This salad can be ready to eat in just two minutes. The cabbage is chopped into tiny pieces and the hummus makes a creamy, high-protein dressing.

SERVES 6–8

1 large, firm cabbage, red *or* white
2 carrots, scrubbed and roughly chopped (optional)
1 onion, sliced (optional)
1 × 300-g/10½-oz tin Hummus
2 tsp cumin seeds
1–2 tbsp soya *or* other milk, if necessary

Remove the outer leaves of the cabbage. Cut the cabbage into quarters and cut out the hardest bits of the core. Cut what is left into smaller pieces, and put it into a food processor bowl. Add the carrot and onion, if using. Pulse until chopped.

Add the hummus and cumin seeds and pulse until they are mixed. Taste and, if the cabbage is a bit dry, add the soya milk. Transfer the salad to a bowl and keep it tightly covered and well packed until you are ready to serve. It tastes best when eaten within an hour of making.

MAIN COURSES

Pistachio Risotto

If curly kale is not in season, try Swiss chard, but slice it and add it together with the peas as it takes less time to cook than kale.

SERVES 2

65 g/2½ oz/½ cup shelled, unsalted pistachios (very fresh if possible; otherwise, refresh in the oven, then cool)
3–4 tbsp olive oil
1 small onion, chopped
220-g/7½-oz packet tofu, cubed (optional)
6–8 tbsp soya milk
4 tbsp water
1 × 440-g/15½-oz tin Organic Ready Rice *or* 3 cups cooked brown rice
2 large stalks curly kale, the leaves chopped into approximately 2.5-cm/1-in squares, the stems into 1-cm/½-in pieces
75 g/3 oz/½ cup frozen peas
2 medium cloves garlic, crushed
sea salt and freshly ground black pepper, to taste

Grind the pistachios to a fine powder in a food processor or coffee grinder and put aside.

Heat a frying pan, then add 2 tablespoons of the oil and fry the onion until it is translucent. Add the tofu cubes, if using, and stir-fry them until they start to colour, adding more oil as necessary.

Add half the milk and all the water and rice, using a fork to break up any lumps of rice. Add the curly kale and steam, covered. Stir after 2 minutes, breaking up any small lumps, and then add the remaining milk, frozen peas and garlic. Cover and steam until the peas are tender (about 2 more minutes). Season well with pepper (and salt if necessary).

Just before serving, tip the ground pistachio nuts over the rice and stir to mix through.

Gram Flour Cumin Pancakes with Ginger Peanut Sauce and Coconut Chutney

This is a party dish inspired by several cuisines: Indian (the chutney), Indonesian (the sauce) and French (the pancakes). The chilli flavour has been reduced to a hint, so that the aromatic coriander, ginger and onion flavours predominate. There are about three hours of work involved, but each element can be prepared in advance. You can make and freeze the pancakes, make the chutney several days in advance and assemble the sauce ingredients ready to be heated in a saucepan. Then, just before serving, chop the red pepper and coriander, reheat the pancakes and put everything into bowls.

Serves 6–8

For the Coconut Chutney
235 g/8¼ oz/3 cups desiccated coconut
450 g/1 lb/2 cups soya or cows' milk yogurt
2 tsp curry powder
2 tsp butter or non-hydrogenated margarine
1 tsp black mustard seeds

For the Gram Flour Cumin Pancakes
350 g/12 oz/3½ cups gram flour (chickpea flour)
1½ tsp sea salt
pinch of cayenne pepper
4 tsp ground cumin
2 tsp ground coriander
750 ml/26 fl oz/3¼ cups water
110 g/4 oz/¾ cup roughly chopped onion
oil, for frying

For the Ginger Peanut Sauce
2-cm/¾-inch piece fresh root ginger, peeled
3 large cloves garlic, peeled
250 g/9 oz/1⅛ cups crunchy peanut butter

Main Courses

½ tsp chilli powder
2 tsp apple juice concentrate
3 tbsp fresh lemon juice
450 ml/14 fl oz/1¾ cups water

For assembling the pancakes
1 large bunch of fresh coriander, washed, dried, stalks removed and leaves chopped
2 red peppers, deseeded and roughly chopped

First, make the chutney by grinding three-quarters of the coconut to a flour in a coffee grinder or food processor. Mix this with the yogurt and the remaining desiccated coconut in a medium-sized bowl. Stir in the curry powder.

Melt the butter or margarine in a frying pan. Add the black mustard seeds and fry them gently until they begin to pop. Remove the pan from the heat quickly so that they do not burn. Stir them into the yogurt mixture and chill the chutney.

Next, make the pancakes. With a food processor, whizz the gram flour, salt, cayenne, cumin and coriander. Add the water and whizz again until smooth. Now add the onion and whizz 3–4 times, so that the onion is lightly chopped, but still in visible pieces. If you are not using a food processor, sift the flour into a bowl and add the spices. Slowly add the water, a few tablespoons at a time, stirring well. Then, finely chop the onion and mix in.

Heat ½ a teaspoon of oil in a crêpe pan over a medium heat until hot. Spoon 4 tablespoons of the batter into the centre of the pan and quickly tilt the pan until the whole surface is covered, as if making a crêpe. When bubbles have formed on the top, turn the pancake over and cook the other side. Each pancake takes about 3–4 minutes to cook (they taste better if they are not too crisp). Continue making the pancakes, adding ½ a teaspoon of oil first each time, until all the batter has been used (you should have 18 pancakes). Place a piece of greaseproof paper between each pancake and pile them up. You can, once they have cooled, put them in a plastic bag and freeze them until needed, defrosting them 30 minutes before using. Refresh them in the oven if the guests are to assemble the dish by hand.

Now, make the sauce. Over a medium-sized saucepan, press the ginger root in a garlic press until all the juice has been extracted, repositioning the ginger several times to do so. Then crush the garlic into the saucepan.

Add the remaining sauce ingredients and stir occasionally over a medium heat until combined and thickened into a homogeneous cream. If it becomes very thick, add a little more water. The sauce burns easily towards the end, so remove it from the heat as soon as it is ready and keep warm.

There are two ways in which you can assemble the dish: the first method tastes better, but relies on keeping the pancakes and sauce warm at the table, while the second method involves assembling the pancakes in advance and keeping them warm in the oven.

For the first method, put all the components on the table, ask guests to spread some sauce (about 2 tablespoons), a dollop of chutney and bits of coriander and red pepper over one side of each pancake, then roll them up.

For the second method, spread only the sauce over the pancakes and roll them up more tightly, then place them on a lightly greased baking tray, cover and heat for 15 minutes in the oven at 150°C/300°F/Gas Mark 2. Then put 2 pancakes on each plate, with a spoonful of Coconut Chutney and some coriander and red pepper on top.

Whichever method you use, serve them with a bitter green salad and green olives or, even better, Moroccan preserved lemons.

Roasted Peppers and Aubergines in a Hummus Crust

Hummus makes a garlicky soft crust that is full of protein and low in fat. Try it with other fillings, but this one, with roasted peppers, grilled aubergines and onions, is delicious warm or at room temperature. Note that if you use something other than Whole Earth hummus, you may find that you will need to add more flour to make a dough that can be handled.

SERVES 4

For the crust
150 g/5 oz/½ heaped cup/½ tin hummus
55 g/2 oz/½ cup wholemeal flour *or* brown rice flour (for those on gluten-free diets)
2 medium cloves garlic, crushed (optional)

For the filling
2 red *or* yellow *or* orange peppers *or* mixed colours
1 medium aubergine
2 tbsp olive oil, plus extra for brushing
sea salt and freshly ground black pepper
1 medium onion
1 tbsp chopped fresh parsley
2 tbsp red wine vinegar *or* balsamic vinegar

Pre-heat the oven to 190°C/375°F/Gas Mark 5 and grease an 18–20-cm/7–8-in pie tin.

Mix the hummus with the flour and garlic, if using. Roll the dough out on a lightly floured board until it is about 5 mm/¼ in thick and use a palette knife to lift it into the prepared tin and trim (the crust can be patted in directly from the mixing bowl, but it does not look as nice). Bake in the pre-heated oven for 20–25 minutes until slightly brown and crisp. At the same time, bake the peppers for the filling, laying them on a baking tray. Turn them after 15 minutes and remove them when the crust is done (see below).

Meanwhile, pre-heat the grill. Wash and slice the aubergine very thinly. Brush with oil and season with salt and pepper. Grill on both sides until soft and slightly charred, then put the slices into a bowl.

Peel and slice the onion thinly, then brush with oil. Grill on both sides until golden brown. Add them to the bowl with the aubergines and add the parsley, too. Add the 2 tablespoons of oil and the vinegar and mix.

When the peppers are slightly charred, remove them from the oven, put them into a plastic bag and seal for a few minutes so the steam loosens the skins. Strip the skins off and cut the peppers into thin strips. Add them to the bowl of vegetables and stir so that the dressing covers them evenly.

Pile the vegetables into the hummus crust and, if serving warm, heat through for 5 minutes in the oven.

Buckwheat Noodles with Jerusalem Artichokes and Toasted Hazelnuts

The toasty taste of Japanese buckwheat noodles is complemented by nutty Jerusalem artichokes and topped with a smooth, savoury sauce. Powdered kelp is available from health food stores and adds a delicious extra flavour.

Serves 4

1 large onion
1 tbsp oil
6 medium Jerusalem artichokes
2 tbsp non-hydrogenated margarine
12 medium mushrooms, sliced
4 celery sticks, sliced
250 g/9 oz Japanese buckwheat noodles (soba)
110 g/4 oz/½ jar Three Nut Butter
2 tsp soy sauce
75 g/3 oz/½ cup toasted hazelnuts, chopped
powdered kelp, to serve (optional)

Slice the onion into thin rings and sauté them in the oil heated in a large frying pan, until they are translucent. Remove them to kitchen paper.

Peel the Jerusalem artichokes and slice them thinly. Melt the margarine in the frying pan and then sauté the artichokes with the sliced mushrooms and celery. Cook until the artichokes have browned and are soft in the centre. Stir in the drained onions.

Meanwhile, cook the noodles according to the directions on the packet, reserving 475 ml/16 fl oz/2 cups of the cooking water before draining and refreshing them with cold water.

When the vegetables are ready, put the Three Nut Butter, reserved cooking water and noodles into a saucepan and heat for about 30 seconds, stirring all the time. Remove from the heat, add the soy sauce and the warm onions and vegetables. Divide between 4 warmed plates and top with the chopped hazelnuts. Offer powdered kelp at the table for your guests to sprinkle on to their taste.

Hummus Pie with Sweet Pepper

Thick Hummus Tahini is delicious combined with fluffy breadcrumbs to make a pie which is crispy on top and will hold its shape when cut.

Serves 4

1 × 300-g/10½-oz tin hummus, drained
1 tin full/1¼ cups fresh wholemeal breadcrumbs (choose the lightest, fluffiest bread — wheat, not rye or sourdough — you can find)
1 tsp dried thyme *or* 1 tbsp ground cumin *or* 1 tsp ground dried rosemary
2 tbsp olive oil, plus 1 tsp for brushing
1 tsp sesame seeds
1 small, red pepper

Pre-heat the oven to 190°C/375°F/Gas Mark 5.

Mix the hummus, breadcrumbs, thyme or cumin or rosemary and 1 tablespoon of the olive oil in a bowl.

Pour 1 tablespoon of the olive oil into a pie plate and roll it around until it covers the plate.

Spread the hummus mixture on the pie plate, sprinkle on the sesame seeds and bake in the pre-heated oven for 10 minutes.

Slice the red pepper into thin rings and then cut them in half again, removing the seeds as you do so. Decorate the top of the pie, pushing the pepper in so it does not stick up. Brush the remaining olive oil over the top and bake for a further 20 minutes.

Leave to rest for 5 minutes, then serve warm or leave to cool completely, chill, then eat at room temperature the next day.

Lotus Leaf Packages

This is a Chinese dim sum recipe adapted for vegans. The lotus leaves subtly perfume the rice and, when they are steaming, fill the house with a marvellous aroma. They are sold loose by weight in Chinese shops and are very inexpensive.

SERVES 4

4 whole Chinese dried mushrooms (optional)
2 large lotus leaves

For the tofu
1 × 220-g/7½-oz packet tofu (roughly chopped)
2 tbsp soy sauce
¼ tsp garlic powder
1 tbsp oil
¼ tsp ground ginger

For the rice
2 × 440-g/15½-oz tins Organic Ready Rice *or* 6 cups cooked brown rice
1 tbsp soy sauce
1 tsp apple juice concentrate
1 tsp toasted sesame oil
110 g/4 oz fresh mushrooms, sliced
oil, for greasing
soy sauce, to serve

fine parcel string
steamer

Soak the dried mushrooms, if using, for 15 minutes, then boil them in the soaking water until they are soft. Slice if necessary.

Soak the lotus leaves in cold water for 15 minutes or until they are pliable, using a glass or plate to keep them underwater. Drain.

To prepare the tofu, dice, then marinate it in the soy sauce for 5 minutes. Sprinkle the garlic powder over the tofu and sauté the tofu until golden brown in the oil. Sprinkle the ginger over it after it has been cooked.

Next, prepare the rice. Empty the tins of rice into a large bowl. Break it up with a fork to separate the grains. Mix in the soy sauce, apple juice concentrate and toasted sesame oil. Add the cooked tofu, fresh and prepared dried mushrooms and mix well.

Bring to the boil 5–8 cm/2–3 in of water in a large saucepan with a steamer. On a large plate or flat surface, generously oil the lotus leaves on their undersides (this is the lighter green side of the leaf). Put half the rice mixture on the greased side of each leaf, fold the edges in over the rice and make 2 neat packages. Tie with string and place in the steamer. Cover and steam for 15 minutes. Open the packages at the table and serve the rice from the leaves with a small saucer of soy sauce for guests to add to taste.

Glass Noodle Salad

This is wonderful as the centrepiece of a summer buffet, as a main course or starter. The noodles, available from oriental shops, are made from mung beans, have an intriguing gelatinous texture and 'cook' in the salad bowl. Noodle salads are common in Asia, here fresh basil is added with toasted sesame seeds and a rich dark dressing to complement the smoked tofu.

SERVES 3

110 g/4 oz bean thread noodles (also called green bean thread or bean vermicelli)
2 tsp vegetable oil
25 g/1 oz dried Chinese mushrooms *or* 10 g/¼ oz dried ceps *or* porcini *or* 3 fresh mushrooms, sliced
1½ tbsp sesame seeds (white hulled ones)
110 g/4 oz smoked tofu
2 spring onions
handful of fresh basil, torn *or* 1½ tsp dried basil

For the sauce
1 tbsp red *or* white wine vinegar
1½ tbsp peanut butter (crunchy is good)
3½ tbsp vegetable oil
1½ tbsp apple juice concentrate
3 small cloves garlic, crushed
4½ tbsp shoyu *or* no-added-sugar soy sauce
freshly ground black pepper
sea salt, if necessary

Unwrap the glass noodles and snip off the strings that bind them. Put them in a medium-sized bowl and pour over 475 ml/16 fl oz/2 cups of boiling water. Leave the noodles to 'cook' for 5 minutes, then slash with a knife or kitchen scissors a few times to cut them into manageable lengths. Leave the noodles to cool for 5 minutes, then drain and toss with the vegetable oil.

Pour boiling water over the dried Chinese mushrooms and soak them for 10 minutes. Drain and cut into strips. If using ceps or porcini, soak them for 10 minutes in warm water, simmer for 15 minutes, then leave to cool.

In a small frying pan, dry roast the sesame seeds until they colour or begin to pop. Remove them from the heat and leave to cool.

Cut the tofu into 2-cm/¾-in squares. Slice the spring onions — the white finely, the green into 2.5-cm/1-in pieces.

Mix the sauce ingredients in a clean screw-top jar by stirring the vinegar and peanut butter together then adding the oil and remaining ingredients and shaking. (If using dried basil rather than fresh, add it to the sauce with the other ingredients.)

Put the mushrooms, smoked tofu and spring onions into the bowl with the noodles and toss (consider keeping aside some of the noodles so your guests can see their translucent texture before adding the sauce). Stir in the sauce and roasted sesame seeds and scatter the fresh basil over the top. Season to taste. Serve at room temperature. (Note that the sauce and sesame seeds can be made in advance, but soak the noodles no more than a few hours before dressing them.)

Green Pea Cakes with Smoky Creole Sauce

Green pea rissoles are soft inside, crunchy on the outside and paired with a smoky tomato sauce, both of which were eagerly scoffed by all who tasted it. This was adapted from a recipe for Lima Bean Cakes from Sheila Ferguson's terrific book, Soul Food *(Weidenfeld and Nicolson, 1989).*

Serves 4

For the Green Pea Cakes
**110 g/4 oz/½ cup green split peas
750 ml/1¼ pints/2 cups water
1 medium onion
75 g/3 oz/1½ cups wholemeal breadcrumbs
2 tbsp chopped fresh parsley
1⅛ tsp salt
¼ tsp cayenne pepper
½ tsp dried sage, ground
vegetable oil, for frying, grilling or baking**

For the Creole Sauce
**1 × 454-g/1-lb jar Italiano spaghetti sauce
½–1 tsp cayenne pepper
1 small, green pepper, seeded and roughly chopped
75 g/3 oz smoked tofu, diced
dash of Tabasco sauce**

First, make the Green Pea Cakes. Bring the split peas to the boil in the water. Skim the froth from the surface, reduce the heat and simmer until the peas are soft (about 40 minutes). Drain well in a sieve.

Measure 275 g/10 oz of the peas. If making by hand, mash the peas, chop the onion and mix in the remaining Green Pea Cakes ingredients, except the oil. If making in a food processor, roughly chop the onion and whizz it, the peas and remaining ingredients together. Taste and add more salt and the remaining peas.

Shape the mixture into 12 round cakes, each about 6 cm/2½ in in diameter and about 2.5 cm/1 in thick. If there is time, refrigerate the pea cakes for an hour.

Now, make the sauce. Put all the ingredients for the sauce into a saucepan and heat until the mixture bubbles. Cook over a low heat for 5 minutes before serving.

Meanwhile, fry the pea cakes. They are best fried in a heavy based frying pan for 3–4 minutes on each side, then drained on kitchen paper. However, they can be brushed with oil and grilled for the same amount of time or baked on a greased baking tray for 12 minutes on each side at 190°C/375°F/Gas Mark 5.

Serve them hot with lots of the sauce and a cool salad.

Smoky Baked Bean Cornbread Pie

This pie has a base of soft cornbread, topped by layers of onions, tarragon, baked beans and smoked tofu. Make it in a large (25 by 30-cm/10 by 12-inch) baking tray or two pie tins.

Serves 6–8

1–2 × 440-g/15½-oz tins no-added-sugar Campfire or Organic baked beans

450 ml/15 fl oz/1⅔ cups liquid from the beans topped up to this amount with soya *or* cows' milk

1 large onion

90 g/3½ oz/⅓ cup non-hydrogenated margarine *or* butter, plus 2 tbsp, for spreading

oil, for greasing and frying

375 g/13 oz/2½ cups fine cornmeal

1 tbsp baking powder

1½ tbsp dried tarragon

½ tsp sea salt

2 tbsp apple juice concentrate

1–2 × 220-g/7½-oz packets smoked tofu (optional, but worth it)

Pre-heat the oven to 200°C/400°F/Gas Mark 6. Open the tins of baked beans and drain the liquid into a measuring jug. Top up to the measure given above with the soya or cows' milk.

Cut the onion in half, then slice thinly and separate into half rings. Set aside.

Melt the 90 g/3½ oz/⅓ cup margarine or butter and set aside. Generously oil the baking tray or pie tins and put them into the oven for 5 minutes (this makes the pies crisp).

Meanwhile, put the cornmeal, baking powder, 1 tablespoon of the tarragon and the salt into a large bowl and mix. Make a well in the centre and add the apple juice concentrate, bean and milk liquid and melted margarine. Combine and immediately pour into the hot tins. Arrange the onion crescents over the top, then bake in the pre-heated oven for 25 minutes.

Meanwhile, slice the smoked tofu in half, then into thin strips and fry these in 2 tablespoons of oil until golden brown. Drain them on kitchen paper. Mix the remaining tarragon with the baked beans. Test the cornbread with a knife to ensure that the centre has cooked (the knife should come out clean, no smears of uncooked dough). Spread the hot cornbread with the remaining margarine or butter, spoon on the beans and cover them with the smoked tofu strips. Cover with foil and seal. Return to the oven for 10–15 minutes until the beans have heated through (if 2 tins of beans were used, cook for 15–20 minutes instead). Serve warm.

Abargoo Rice

This aromatic Persian dish was served to Craig Sams in a village called Abargoo in Southern Iran in 1965 and is adapted from his Macrobiotic Brown Rice Cook Book *(Inner Traditions, 1993).*

SERVES 2 AS A MAIN COURSE, 4 AS AN ACCOMPANIMENT

1 × 440-g/15½-oz tin Organic Ready Rice *or* 3 cups cooked brown rice
2½ tbsp olive oil
40 g/1½ oz/⅓ cup pine nuts
40 g/1½ oz/⅓ cup almonds, chopped
40 g/1½ oz/⅓ cup sultanas
85 ml/3 fl oz/⅓ cup water
¼ tsp cinnamon
tiny pinch of ground cloves
sea salt and freshly ground black pepper

In a large frying pan with a lid, first lightly steam the rice by using a collapsible steamer. Fork over the grains until they separate. Remove the steamer with the rice, spill out any water left in the pan and dry it.

Heat the olive oil briefly in the pan, then add the pine nuts and chopped almonds, and fry until lightly browned (they burn easily so watch them carefully).

Spill the rice into the pan and add the remaining ingredients, except the sea salt and pepper. Cover and simmer for 2 minutes. Add salt and pepper to taste. Serve hot, lukewarm or cold.

Apricot Pilaf

This delicious pilaf rice is flavoured with allspice and apricots. The risotto in the variation is ready in under ten minutes and yet it has the consistency and bite a risotto should have — slightly wet, with firm plump grains.

Serves 4

300 g/11 oz/1½ cups brown rice (long grain if possible)
600 ml/1 pint/2½ cups water
pinch of sea salt
½ tsp ground allspice
6 tbsp apricot pure fruit spread
1 tbsp non-hydrogenated margarine *or* oil, plus 1 tsp (optional)
2 tbsp pine nuts
4 tbsp blanched split almonds (optional)
2–4 tbsp unsalted pistachios (optional)
4 tbsp sultanas

Pick over and wash the rice under cold, running water until it runs clear. Put the measured water and rice into a large saucepan and bring to the boil, skimming away any froth that forms. Add the salt, allspice and apricot spread, mix well, reduce the heat, cover and simmer *very* gently until the water has been absorbed (45–50 minutes). Try to resist taking a peek as it tastes best when undisturbed, but check during the last 5 minutes that it is not sticking.

Meanwhile, heat the margarine or oil in a frying pan and quickly fry the pine nuts, almonds and pistachios, if using, and sultanas until lightly coloured.

When the rice has cooked, add the nuts and sultanas and stir. The 1 tsp of margarine can be stirred in at this point, if liked. Serve warm.

Variation: Apricot Risotto

Start by frying the nuts and sultanas in a large saucepan and remove. Empty the contents of 440-g/15½-oz/tin of Organic Ready Rice (3 cups) into the pan, followed by 4 tbsp apricot pure fruit spread, 4 tbsp water and ¼ tsp ground allspice. Bring to the boil, then reduce the heat to very low. Cover and stir occasionally until the water has been absorbed (2–3 minutes). Stir in the nuts and sultanas. Serves 2–3 people, or even 4 as a starter.

Baked Bean Pancakes

These thick pancakes have a delicious soft centre and brown crust that will appeal to the whole family. They are ideal for a quick supper or even a festive breakfast.

MAKES ABOUT 20

150 g/5 oz/1¼ cups wholemeal flour
½ tsp bicarbonate of soda
¼ tsp sea salt
150 ml/5 fl oz/⅝ cup water
1 × 440-g/15½-oz tin no-added-sugar Organic or Campfire baked beans
1 small onion, chopped
1 green pepper, seeded and chopped (optional)
2 tbsp chopped fresh coriander or parsley (optional)
2 tsp curry powder (optional)
½ tsp chilli powder (optional)
oil, for frying

greaseproof paper

In a medium-sized bowl, mix the flour, bicarbonate of soda and salt. Add the water and mix it in lightly. Stir in the tin of beans with all of its liquid, and the onion. Add the green pepper, if using, and/or coriander or parsley, if using, and curry powder and/or chilli powder, if using.

Heat a heavy based frying pan or griddle and add a little oil. As soon as it sizzles spoon a dollop of the mixture on, spreading it with the back of the spoon to the thickness of the baked beans. You can make the pancakes any size you like, but about 10 cm/4 in in diameter is the easiest size to handle. When bubbles show through on the top, turn it over to cook the other side. Keep the first pancakes warm in the oven until they are all cooked, inserting a piece of greaseproof paper between each one as you pile them up.

Ketchup and Mustard Burgers

A well-flavoured pink burger on a bun that is both sustaining and sustainable.

MAKES 8

1 small onion
1 × 425-g/15-oz tin kidney beans without added sugar, drained *or* 250 g/9 oz/1½ cups cooked kidney beans
225 g/8 oz/½ tin Organic Ready Rice *or* 1½ cups cooked brown rice
2½ tbsp no-added-sugar ketchup
1 tsp garlic powder
2 tsp brown rice vinegar
1 tsp organic mild mustard
1 tsp dried oregano
¼ tsp dried sage, ground
pinch of dried thyme
¼ tsp sea salt, or more, to taste
1 tbsp sesame seeds
2 tbsp oil

TO SERVE
8 wholemeal burger buns, baps *or* pitta bread, warmed
lettuce
tomato slices
thin slices of mild onion (optional)
ketchup
mustard

In a food processor, chop the onion, half the kidney beans and half the rice. Add all the remaining ingredients, except the oil, and combine well. Now add the remaining kidney beans and rice and whizz for just a short time allowing some of the pieces to remain whole for texture.

Heat a large, heavy based frying pan and add half the vegetable oil. Drop a heaped tablespoonful of mixture into the pan and flatten to make a burger 1 cm/½ in thick. Fry 4 burgers at a time over a medium heat, turning several times until they have cooked through and are crisp on the outside.

Halve the warmed wholemeal buns, baps or pitta bread. Add the lettuce, sliced tomato and mild onion, if using. Put the hot burgers inside and serve with more ketchup and mustard.

Golden Rice Burgers

These golden-flecked vegeburgers are light, tasting of carrots, sesame seeds and whatever herb you choose.

MAKES 12 — 76g each

200 g/7 oz/1¼ cups sesame seeds *or* sesame seeds and unsalted nuts
1 tbsp olive oil
200 g/7 oz carrots, sliced
1 medium onion, chopped
225 g/8 oz/1½ cups Organic Ready Rice (½ tin) *or* cooked brown rice
200 g/7 oz no-added-sugar Organic or Campfire baked beans, juice drained off
3 tbsp organic ketchup
1 tsp dried rosemary *or* other herb
4 tbsp wholemeal flour
oil, for greasing

In a large frying pan, dry roast the sesame seeds or sesame seeds and nuts. Remove them to the bowl of a food processor. Add the olive oil to a frying pan and sauté the carrots and onions until they have browned slightly.

Add the rice to the frying pan, break up any lumps and sauté briefly for a minute or two.

Pre-heat the oven to 190°C/375°F/Gas Mark 5.

Meanwhile, add the baked beans to the food processor and whizz with the sesame seeds and nuts. Now add the contents of the frying pan and ketchup and whizz. Add the rosemary or other herb and flour and pulse 2–3 times. Remove the sharp blade.

Grease a large baking tray. Form 12 burgers, each about 9 cm/3½ in in diameter and bake for 25–30 minutes. Serve warm or cold. These burgers freeze well, too.

Hummus Pizza with Fresh Herbs

Both hummus and baked beans make excellent pizza toppings. Prepared organic pizza bases are now available, but a home-made pizza can still be ready in 1½ hours and does not require much effort.

SERVES 4

For the base
65 ml/2½ fl oz/⅓ cup water
¼ tsp dried yeast
¼ tsp apple juice concentrate *or* grain syrup
110 g/4 oz/1 cup strong wholemeal bread flour
pinch of sea salt
1 tbsp olive oil, plus extra for greasing
2 tsp chopped fresh single *or* mixed herbs (e.g., basil, tarragon, oregano or dill)

For the topping
1 × 300-g/10.5-oz tin hummus
2–3 cloves garlic, crushed
1 tbsp chopped fresh *or* 1 tsp dried oregano *or* thyme
4 medium tomatoes, sliced or chopped
1 tbsp olive oil

Choice of further toppings
1 onion, thinly sliced
black or green olives
4–6 mushrooms, sliced
1 green pepper, sliced
1 tbsp capers
2–4 tbsp pine nuts
1–2 tbsp pumpkin seeds

Boil the water and leave to cool to 'blood heat' (this is when you can put a finger in comfortably without having to snatch it away but before it is lukewarm). Sprinkle the dried yeast on top and stir in the apple juice concentrate or grain syrup. Leave for 10–15 minutes until a thick froth appears on top.

Mix the flour, salt, olive oil and herbs in a large bowl or food processor. Add the yeast and water and mix until a smooth dough is formed that comes away from the sides of the bowl cleanly. You do not have to knead this dough if you are pressed for time, although kneading produces a softer crust. If you do knead it, do so for about 10 minutes by hand, or 2 minutes with a kneading attachment in a food processor. Cover the surface of the dough with a little oil and put it into a bowl. Wrap a clean tea towel around the bowl and put it in a warm place. Leave it until the dough has risen (20–60 minutes).

Pre-heat the oven to 220°C/425°F/Gas Mark 7.

When the dough has risen, pat it flat, then roll it and stretch it into a greased 23–25-cm/9–10-in tin. Brush a light layer of olive oil over the surface of the dough. Bake without the topping in the pre-heated oven for 10 minutes.

Drain off any liquid from the hummus, then mix in the garlic and herbs. Spread a few slices of tomato on the partially cooked base, then a layer of the hummus mixture. On top, scatter more slices of tomato and some or all of the further toppings. Sprinkle the olive oil over the top and bake for a further 15–20 minutes or until the base is just lightly browned.

Variation: Baked Bean Pizza with Thyme, Onions and Green Peppers

Prepare the base as above, then after baking the base for 10 minutes, spread 1 tbsp of organic ketchup over it. Lay some slices of onion over this. Pour off most of the liquid from a 440-g/15½-oz tin of Organic baked beans, mix in 1 tsp dried thyme and spread this over the base. Add slices of green peppers and cook for 15 more minutes.

Hot Tamale Pie

In the base of this pie are traditional Mexican refried beans (which here are not actually fried twice). In the centre is SuperSpread 'cheese', which mimics melted cheese very well, or cheese, and, on top, is a crispy cornmeal, tamale crust. Served warm, the other 'hot' is up to you. Chillies can be added to the cornmeal crust or the beans or everything!

SERVES 4–6

For the refried beans
250 g/9 oz/1¼ cups pinto beans *or* kidney beans
1 tomato, chopped
½ green pepper, seeded and chopped
2 tbsp chopped onion
2 cloves garlic, crushed
salt to taste

For the 'cheese'
6 tbsp SuperSpread
40 g/1½ oz/¾ cup Engevita nutritional yeast flakes (Marigold)
or 6 tbsp grated cheese, if preferred

For the tamale topping
100 g/3½ oz/1 cup fine cornmeal
1–2 tbsp fresh green chillies, chopped (optional)
½ tsp sea salt
1 tbsp SuperSpread *or* oil
1 tsp barley malt *or* other grain syrup
250 ml/8 fl oz/1 cup boiling water
Tabasco sauce *or* chopped fresh chillies, to taste (optional)

Pick over and wash the beans. Soak them overnight or cover with water in a large saucepan, bring them to the boil, boil for 2 minutes, turn off the heat and cover for 1 hour. Drain.

Put the soaked beans into a large saucepan, then add water to cover by 2.5 cm/1 in, bring to the boil and boil rapidly for 10 minutes. Then reduce the heat and simmer gently until cooked (45 minutes to 1 hour). Drain, if necessary, then mash with a fork or in a food processor. Mix in the tomato, green pepper, onion and garlic, taste and add a little salt if necessary.

Pre-heat the oven to 200°C/400°F/Gas Mark 6. Spoon the bean mixture into 4 large or 6 small ramekins or a 20–23-cm/8–9-in pan. Mix the 'cheese' ingredients and divide this between the ramekins or spread over the top of the pan.

Make the tamale topping next by mixing the cornmeal with the chillies, if using, and the salt, stirring in the SuperSpread or oil and barley malt or grain syrup and beating in the boiling water, until the lumps have disappeared. Drop the mixture in spoonfuls over the 'cheese' then gently spread it so that the 'cheese' is covered. Bake in the pre-heated oven for 25–30 minutes until the crust is lightly brown.

Ten-Minute Vegetable Stew Italiano

Great when you are hungry and would like something substantial quickly. Use any vegetables you have if you have no courgettes or green peppers to hand.

Serves 4

2 large onions, halved and sliced
2 medium courgettes *or* half a cucumber, roughly diced
1 large green pepper, seeded and roughly diced
2–3 cloves garlic, crushed *or* sliced
1 × 220-g/7½-oz packet smoked tofu, roughly chopped (optional)
1 × 440-g/15½-oz/3 cups/tin Organic Ready Rice (optional)
1 × 454-g/1-lb jar Italiano or Mushroom Italiano spaghetti sauce
250 ml/8 fl oz/1 cup water
3tbsp pine nuts (optional if not using smoked tofu)

Put all of the prepared vegetables, garlic, smoked tofu, if using, and Ready Rice in a large saucepan and cover with the Italiano sauce. Add the water and heat gently, stirring regularly, for 7–10 minutes. Fork through the rice to break up the lumps.

Sprinkle the pine nuts on top, if using. Serve on bulgur or couscous if not using Ready Rice.

Quick and Different Baked Beans

The best recipe for baked beans may be to open the tin, and eat, but to ring the changes, try the following recipes. This Hot-and-Sour recipe was a big success with tasters.

Hot and Sour Baked Beans

SERVES 2–3

2 tbsp oil
1 onion, chopped
2 cloves garlic, crushed
1 slice fresh root ginger, grated
1 green pepper, seeded and chopped
1 × 440-g/15½-oz tin no-added-sugar Organic or Campfire baked beans
3 slices tinned pineapple in natural juice, or equivalent, drained and cut into chunks
1 tsp soy sauce
2 tbsp apple juice concentrate
1 tsp chilli powder
1 tsp toasted sesame oil

Heat the oil and sauté the onion, garlic, ginger and green peppers for about 3 minutes. Add the remaining ingredients, stir and cook until the pineapple is hot.

Variation: Simple Curried Beans
Add 1 teaspoon of curry powder, or more to taste, for every tin of baked beans before heating them.

Quick Chilli

This recipe can also be used as a filling for tacos, enchilladas or burritos.

SERVES 4

1 × 125-g/4-oz packet Vegeburger™ mix by Realeat
120 ml/4 fl oz/½ cup water
2 tbsp oil
½ medium onion, chopped
1 clove garlic, crushed
½ green pepper, seeded and chopped
1 × 440-g/15½-oz tin no-added-sugar Organic or Campfire baked beans
3–5 fresh tomatoes *or* 1 × 400-g/14-oz tin plum tomatoes
1 tsp chilli powder
pinch of cayenne pepper
1 tsp ground cumin
1 tsp dried oregano
250 ml/8 fl oz/1 cup water (half this if serving in taco shells)
handful of chopped fresh coriander leaves *or* shredded lettuce and lemon juice, to garnish

Mix the Vegeburger mix with the water and half the oil and leave to soak for 15 minutes.

In a medium-sized saucepan, lightly sauté the onion and garlic together for 3 minutes. Add the green pepper and cook for 1 more minute. Mix in the baked beans and remaining ingredients, including the Vegeburger mix, and simmer for 7–10 minutes.

Garnish with the coriander leaves and serve with rice or in a warmed taco shell with shredded lettuce tossed in lemon juice.

Hot Grilled Sandwiches

The first, useful, recipe is a variation of baked beans on toast. If you are making this for children, they may prefer less onion and cayenne.

SERVES 1

2 tbsp no-added-sugar Organic or Campfire baked beans, without liquid
1 tsp SuperSpread *or* mayonnaise
1 tsp finely chopped onion
pinch cayenne pepper *or* curry powder
1 slice wholemeal bread

Mash the beans lightly with a fork, then mix in the remaining ingredients, except the bread. Lightly toast one side of the bread, then spread the bean mixture over the untoasted side and grill until the edges of the bread are toasted.

Variations

Top a slice of bread with peanut butter and apricot pure fruit spread or put this inside a pitta bread and grill.

Mix 1 tablespoon peanut butter, 1 teaspoon chopped onion and 1 teaspoon mashed smoked tofu, spread on a slice of bread and grill.

Mix 1 tablespoon peanut butter, 1 teaspoon sultanas and a pinch of ground cinnamon (optional), spread on a slice of bread and grill.

Spread 1 tablespoon peanut butter on toast, add a sliced banana and grill.

Spread 1 tablespoon Savoury Nut Butter on a piece of bread, top with chopped spring onion and tomato slices and grill.

Spread 1 tablespoon Savoury Nut Butter on a piece of bread, scatter a little chopped spring onion, cucumber and a few drops of brown rice vinegar over the top and grill.

Spread 1 tablespoon Three Nut Butter on a piece of bread and a thin layer of maize syrup on top and grill.

Rice and Peas

A quick version of the traditional West Indian dish, this can be ready in ten minutes. It is a comforting and well-flavoured mix, taste-tested by a Jamaican friend, Olivia Brown, for authenticity. Although she uses tinned beans, she did not approve of it all being so easy — 'Rice from a tin?!', she said.

SERVES 4

1 × 425-g/15-oz tin no-added-sugar kidney beans *or* pigeon peas, gunga peas *or* black-eyed peas (approximately 250 g/9 oz/1½ cups cooked beans)
1 medium onion
1 × 450-g/15½-oz tin Organic Ready Rice *or* 3 cups cooked rice, dry and slightly salted
1 clove garlic, crushed
¼ tsp dried thyme
15 g/½ oz coconut cream from a block
1 medium tomato, roughly chopped
sea salt

Open the tin of kidney beans and pour off the liquid into a measuring jug. Add sufficient water to make the liquid up to 150 ml/5 fl oz/½ cup. Add the beans and the liquid to a medium-sized saucepan.

Chop the onion and add it to the saucepan. Turn on the heat to high, add the remaining ingredients, except the salt, and stir to break up the rice. When it is boiling, reduce the heat and simmer until the onion is soft and the liquid has been absorbed (about 5 minutes). Taste and add a little salt if necessary. Serve warm. To reheat any leftovers, add 1 tablespoon of water and cook over a very low heat.

Herby, Creamy Rice Loaf

Amazingly, no egg is needed to hold this light, grain and tofu mixture together. Try it with your choice of fresh green herbs. If you use a tin of Organic Ready Rice, the loaf can be in the oven in 20 minutes.

SERVES 6–8

150 g/5 oz/1 cup uncooked bulgur
350 ml/12 fl oz/1½ cups water
1 small onion
1 small carrot
1 × 220-g/7½-oz packet tofu, drained
1 × 440-g/15½-oz tin Organic Ready Rice *or* 3 cups cooked rice
1 tbsp fresh herbs *or* 1 tsp dried (tarragon, sage, thyme or dill are good)
3 tbsp tahini
4 tbsp soy *or* shoyu sauce
2 tbsp Kensington Sauce (optional)
1 tbsp arrowroot
vegetable oil, for greasing
1 tbsp dark miso

Pre-heat the oven to 180°C/350°F/Gas Mark 4. Cook the bulgur in a large-sized saucepan by adding the water, bringing it to the boil, then simmering it for 10–15 minutes until it is fluffy.

Meanwhile, chop the onion and carrot and mash the tofu.

When the bulgur is nearly cooked, add the rice, breaking it up and mix them together. Remove the pan from the heat and add the onion, carrot, herbs, tahini, soy or shoyu sauce and Kensington Sauce, if using. Sprinkle the arrowroot over the mixture and stir it in. Add the mashed tofu and mix it in well.

Half fill the kettle and put it on to boil.

Cover the bottom of a greased medium-sized loaf tin with a rectangle of greaseproof paper, then grease again. Alternatively, use a round 20-cm/8-in, high-sided cake tin and prepare it in the same way.

Pile the mixture into the prepared tin, smooth the top, then mix the miso with 85 ml/3 fl oz of the boiled water and pour it over the loaf. Lay a piece of greaseproof paper over the mixture, just covering the edges.

Put the loaf or cake tin into a large baking tin. Carefully, pour boiling water into the larger pan to reach halfway up the sides of the loaf or cake tin, then put it into the pre-heated oven and bake for 1 hour. Let it cool for 10–20 minutes before turning it out and cutting it into slices. Serve it warm with a green salad or at room temperature the next day.

Savoury Tchease Spread

This spread teases the taste buds' memory of matured cheese, although the texture is soft. It can be heated without loss of flavour, but is best fresh in a sandwich with, perhaps, a thin slice of mild onion or a few drops of Tabasco sauce. This was a serendipitous discovery that is now a firm favourite.

SERVES 4

75 g/3 oz firm tofu
2 tbsp Savoury Nut Butter

Mash the ingredients together well or do this in a food processor. Keep chilled and use within 2 days.

Variation

For a near approximation of the above, mix 2 tablespoons peanut butter, plus ¼ teaspoon yeast extract.

Potato Buckwheat and Dill Casserole

The layers of sliced potatoes, buckwheat, onions and green pepper in a peanut butter sauce make a savoury casserole for a winter evening.

Serves 6

oil, for greasing
750 g/1½ lb/4 cups potatoes, very thinly sliced
90 g/3½ oz/½ cup buckwheat, toasted *or* untoasted, rinsed
1 green pepper, seeded and roughly chopped
2 medium onions, chopped
750 ml/1¼ pints/3 cups water
110 g/4 oz/½ cup crunchy peanut butter
3 tbsp shoyu *or* soy sauce
1 tsp dried dill weed
2 tbsp fresh wholemeal breadcrumbs, for topping

Pre-heat the oven to 180°C/350°F/Gas Mark 4. Grease a large deep casserole with oil.

Put half the sliced potatoes in the bottom. Then sprinkle the buckwheat over. Scatter the green pepper on next, then the onions. Top with the remaining sliced potatoes.

Mix some of the water with the peanut butter and add in the shoyu or soy sauce and dill weed. Stir in the remaining water until the peanut butter has dissolved and pour this over the top of the casserole. Cover and bake in the pre-heated oven for 45–50 minutes or until the buckwheat has cooked. Sprinkle on the breadcrumbs and cook uncovered for 5 more minutes until they have lightly browned.

Mushroom and Peanut Stew with Cabbage 'Noodles'

This is a useful and well-flavoured one-dish meal that can be made from bare essentials for a quick supper. The cabbage cooks down, loses its taste and looks like long thin noodles.

SERVES 4–6

6 tbsp vegetable oil
4 medium onions, chopped
4 small cloves garlic, crushed
110 g/4 oz/1 cup whole raw *or* roasted peanuts (optional)
2 tbsp dried basil
1 tbsp ground cumin
1 tbsp garam masala
1 tbsp ground coriander
2 medium potatoes, finely diced
1 × 454-g/1-lb jar/1¾ cups Italiano spaghetti sauce
300 ml/10 fl oz/1¼ cups water
450 g/1 lb/1 cup savoy or spring cabbage, very thinly sliced
100–225 g/4–8 oz mushrooms, sliced
sea salt
500 g/1¼ lb yogurt or grain of your choice, cooked, to serve

Heat a third of the oil in a very large saucepan. Sauté the onions, garlic and peanuts, if using, until tender.

Add the remaining oil, herbs, spices and potatoes and sauté for 2 more minutes.

Add the Italiano sauce and water. Add the cabbage and mushrooms and bring to the boil. Reduce the heat, cover, then simmer until the potatoes are tender (10–15 minutes). Stir occasionally to keep it from sticking. Taste at the end of the cooking time and add a little salt if necessary.

Serve with the yogurt on top or with cooked rice, millet or bulgur.

Spinach Noodle Bake with Thyme and Tarragon

This casserole makes a satisfying and filling one-dish meal because it contains as many vegetables as noodles. The sweet taste of spinach and broad beans is brought out by the mild and creamy peanut, thyme and tarragon sauce.

Serves 6–8

225 g/8 oz wholemeal noodles *or* pasta shapes
450 g/1 lb spinach *or* 750 g/1½ lb if not using broad beans
2 tbsp oil
2 large onions, cut in half and sliced
½ tsp sea salt
225 g/8 oz baby broad beans (optional)
475 ml/16 fl oz/2 cups soya milk
200 g/7 oz/¾ cup peanut butter (smooth, preferably)
1 tbsp dried *or* 1¾ tbsp fresh thyme
1 tbsp dried *or* 1¾ tbsp fresh tarragon
1 tbsp sesame seeds *or* wheatgerm *or* wholemeal breadcrumbs

If you have a large flameproof casserole the whole dish can be made in one pot, including boiling the pasta. If you do not have such a dish, cook the pasta in boiling salted water until it is barely tender, then rinse and drain.

Meanwhile, wash the spinach in several changes of water and trim off any brown bits. Heat the oil and sauté the onion until it is limp (3–5 minutes). Cut the spinach into 2.5-cm/1-in strips with scissors into the pan and cook, uncovered, until it cooks down (about 5 minutes). Season with the salt.

Meanwhile, steam the broad beans, if using, for about 4 minutes or until just cooked, then mix them with the spinach.

Pre-heat the oven to 190°C/375°F/Gas Mark 5.

To the spinach and broad beans, add the soya milk, peanut butter, thyme and tarragon and cook, stirring, until the peanut butter dissolves. Add the cooked pasta and mix well, adding a little more salt if needed. If you are using a flameproof casserole, wipe any sauce from the edges. Otherwise, spoon the mixture into a greased casserole. Sprinkle with the sesame seeds, wheatgerm or breadcrumbs, then bake, uncovered, in the pre-heated oven for 20 minutes.

MAIN COURSES

Cauliflower Please

This casserole, with its thick, rich, savoury sauce baked over cauliflower, is as warming and satisfying as the classic cauliflower cheese on which it is based.

SERVES 4–6

1 large cauliflower (approximately 1.5–1.75 kg/3–4 lb)
2 tbsp non-hydrogenated margarine *or* SuperSpread *or* butter
110 g/4 oz/½ cup smooth peanut butter
2 tbsp wholemeal flour
½ tsp sea salt
freshly ground black pepper
½ tsp ground coriander (optional, but recommended)
600 ml/1 pint/2½ cups soya *or* cows' milk
2 tbsp sesame seeds *or* breadcrumbs *or* wheatgerm

Wash and trim the cauliflower, reserving the greens. Break it into florets, then chop the greens.

Steam the cauliflower and greens, covered, in 5 cm/2 in of boiling water for 5–7 minutes until nearly cooked.

Pre-heat the oven to 180°C/350°F/Gas Mark 4.

Meanwhile, mix the margarine or SuperSpread or butter with the peanut butter in a small saucepan over a medium heat. Then, add the flour, salt, pepper to taste and coriander. Gradually add the milk, stirring until the mixture begins to boil. Reduce the heat and simmer for 1 minute — the sauce should be nice and thick.

Drain the cauliflower, put it into a casserole dish and pour the sauce over. Sprinkle the sesame seeds, breadcrumbs or wheatgerm over the top and bake, uncovered, in the pre-heated oven for 15 minutes.

Variation
Savoury Nut Butter can be used instead of peanut butter for a more robust sauce, but if you do, leave out the ground coriander.

Smoked Tofu with Barbecue Sauce

Here is a good imitation of American-style barbecued spare ribs. The barbecue sauce is Sheila Ferguson's, taken from Soul Food, (Wiedenfeld & Nicolson, 1989) and is authentic (except for the substitution for the sugar) and can be used on anything. This is a great dish for family occasions, and there is no need to go outside to grill these either as it is all done in the oven.

SERVES 4–6

For the sauce
1 tbsp vegetable oil
1 small onion, finely chopped
1½ tsp cider vinegar
4 tbsp organic brown rice syrup *or* half brown rice syrup, half apple juice concentrate
1 tsp mustard powder
1½ tsp celery salt *or* ½ tsp celery seeds
pinch of cayenne pepper
½ tsp paprika
120 g/4½ oz/½ cup organic no-added-sugar ketchup
1½ tbsp Kensington Sauce *or* vegan Worcestershire Sauce
2 tbsp lemon juice
120 ml/4 fl oz/½ cup water

For the tofu
3 × 220-g/7½-oz packets smoked tofu
oil, for frying
garlic powder

First make the sauce. In a saucepan, heat the oil and sauté the chopped onion in it for 5 minutes. Add in all the remaining sauce ingredients and mix well. Bring to the boil, then simmer, uncovered, over a low heat for 20 minutes. (You can make this several days in advance, or freeze it.)

Drain the smoked tofu and press it between sheets of kitchen paper until it is dry. Cut it into 2.5-cm/1-in cubes and marinate them in the sauce for 30 minutes to 1 hour or longer.

Pre-heat the oven to 180°C/350°F/Gas Mark 4. Heat 2–3 tablespoons of oil in a heavy based frying pan. Remove the tofu from the sauce, scraping off any large bits of onion. Fry the cubes on each side until just lightly browned, no darker. Lift them into an oiled baking tin without draining. Only make 1 layer of tofu with spaces in between (2 tins may be necessary). Sprinkle garlic powder liberally on all sides.

Pour the sauce over the tofu in a thin layer, leaving the tofu partly exposed. The sauce should not reach the full height of the tofu. Bake in the pre-heated oven, uncovered for 30 minutes, or until the sauce has gone slightly sticky. Serve warm, in small portions with several salads as accompaniments.

Oil-Free Stir-Fried Vegetables with Toasted Hazelnuts

Dieters will enjoy this stir-fry just as much without the toasted hazelnuts.

SERVES 2 AS A MAIN COURSE, 4 AS AN ACCOMPANIMENT

25 g/1 oz/3 tbsp hazelnuts *or* cashews
2 carrots, thinly sliced
2–3 tbsp Reduced Calorie Oil Free Vinaigrette
1 courgette, thickly sliced
2 celery sticks, thinly sliced
110 g/4 oz mange-tout, trimmed, if necessary
110 g/4 oz mushrooms, sliced (optional)
110 g/4 oz tofu, sliced (optional)
2–3 spring onions

In a heavy based frying pan over a low heat, first, dry roast the nuts until they are golden brown. Remove them to a plate to crisp up as they cool.

Over a medium heat, add the carrots and 1 tablespoon of the vinaigrette and stir until coated and the liquid evaporates and cooks the carrots. Add the rest of the vegetables and tofu, a further tablespoon of vinaigrette and stir until cooked. Add a further tablespoon if the vegetables are sticking too much. Toss in the nuts and serve.

VEGETABLE SIDE DISHES

Mashed Potatoes with Grilled Corn, Garlic and Dill

Grilling corn concentrates and slightly caramelizes its flavour, and here, it is further brought out by the mild mustard in the mashed potatoes. This is a potato dish that really does not need salt.

Serves 4

450 g/1 lb potatoes, quartered
4 tsp olive oil, or more to taste, plus extra for brushing
2 corn cobs, with leaves removed
2 cloves garlic, chopped
2 tbsp mild organic mustard
few sprigs fresh or freeze-dried dill weed, to garnish

Boil the quartered potatoes in sufficient water to cover for 20 minutes until soft. Drain and mash.

Meanwhile, pre-heat the grill. Also, brush olive oil over the corn cobs and lay them in a flat heatproof or flameproof dish. Grill the corn slowly, turning from time to time, and remove when golden. You can lightly roast the chopped garlic at the same time. Slice the corn kernels off the cob.

Add the mustard, 4 tablespoons of olive oil and the garlic to the mashed potatoes. Top with the corn kernels, garnish with the dill and serve.

Spinach Soufflés

Chopped spinach soufflés made regular appearances at my mother's table and here the idea is adapted for vegan cooking. These are an unusual way to enjoy spinach and make a novelty extra vegetable for a large meal. Otherwise, it is easy to eat two soufflés each, so if you anticipate this happening, simply double the recipe.

Makes 4

225 g/8 oz fresh spinach
50 g/2 oz/¼ cup smooth peanut butter
120 ml/4 fl oz/½ cup soya milk
1 tbsp wholemeal flour
½ tsp arrowroot
1½ tsp baking powder
¼ tsp sea salt
pinch of freshly grated nutmeg
oil, for greasing

Pre-heat the oven to 190°C/375°F/Gas Mark 5.

Wash the spinach thoroughly. Trim off and discard the stems and any damaged parts. Finely chop and weigh the leaves: you should have 150 g/5 oz. Add the spinach and the rest of the ingredients except the oil, to a food processor, and mix them together (if a food processor is not used, it may be necessary to heat the peanut butter and milk in order to mix them easily). Do not worry that there is not much liquid binding the chopped spinach.

Grease 4 ramekins with a little oil, then spoon the mixture into them and bake in the pre-heated oven for 35–40 minutes, or until a knife inserted comes out clean.

Parsnips in Creamy Dressing

Mild mustard is a good foil for parsnips and, here, they are served with a yogurt dressing that is delicious either warm or at room temperature.

SERVES 4

4 medium parsnips, well-scrubbed and sliced

For the dressing
120 ml/4 fl oz/½ cup soya or cows' milk yogurt
2 tsp mild organic mustard
1 tsp apple juice concentrate (or 2 tsp if using a strong cows' milk yogurt)

Put 2.5 cm/1 in of water into a medium-sized saucepan and bring to the boil. Add the parsnips, cover, and steam until tender.

Meanwhile, mix the ingredients for the dressing. Remove the parsnips to a warmed plate and spoon the dressing over them.

Sweet Potatoes and Plums

There are two types of sweet potato: some have orange centres and some white. The organic ones are usually orange and are now increasingly available. They have a delicate taste, which is brought out by Golden Plum pure fruit spread in this recipe. For the white ones, cook as below and mash with soya milk and pepper, then serve with a dollop of apricot pure fruit spread.

SERVES 4

2 large or 4 medium orange sweet potatoes, scrubbed
4 tbsp Golden Plum pure fruit spread

Drop the unpeeled sweet potatoes in the boiling water to cover and cook, covered, for 20 minutes, or until tender. Drain, and leave them to cool a bit until they are easy to handle.

Peel them, return them to the pan and mash coarsely. Add the Golden Plum pure fruit spread, heat through and serve immediately.

… VEGETABLE SIDE DISHES …

Two Ways to Glaze Carrots

Here are two delicious recipes for glazed carrots. The slow cooking perks up the carrots' flavour and the slightly sweet flavourings bring out the carrots' natural sweetness.

Sweet Lemon Carrots

SERVES 4

4 tbsp water
120 ml/4 fl oz/½ cup Real Lemonade
225 g/8 oz/2 cups carrots, thinly sliced
2 tbsp non-hydrogenated margarine *or* butter

In a small saucepan, bring the water and Real Lemonade to the boil. Add the carrots and margarine or butter. Cover and simmer until the liquid has nearly all been absorbed (about 20 minutes). Leave to cool for a minute or two, then serve.

Carrots or Swede in Apricot Mustard Sauce

3 tbsp apricot pure fruit spread
4 tbsp water
225 g/8 oz/2 cups carrots, thinly sliced *or* swede cut into 2.5-cm/1-in cubes
1 tbsp non-hydrogenated margarine *or* butter
½ tsp hot Dijon mustard *or* mild organic mustard

In a small saucepan, bring the apricot spread and water to the boil. Add the carrots or swede and margarine or butter. Cover and simmer for 12–15 minutes, or until they are cooked, stirring regularly.

Remove the pan from the heat and stir in the mustard. Serve hot or at room temperature.

Cabbage with Marmalade and Juniper Berries

Both marmalade and the mixed berry variation enhance lightly cooked cabbage, lifting it from the school dinner to dinner party fare.

SERVES 4–6
½ tsp juniper berries, crushed
550 g/1¼ lb cabbage, thinly sliced
140 g/5 oz/½ cup no-added-sugar marmalade

In a large saucepan, bring 1 cm/½ in water to the boil with the crushed juniper berries.

Add the sliced cabbage and boil, covered, for 2 minutes, or until it has softened, but is still crunchy. Pour off the water (saving it for soups, or drink it warm for the vitamins).

Mix in the marmalade, heat it through, then serve immediately.

Variation
Leave out the juniper berries and marmalade and use 200 g/7 oz/¾ cup Mixed Berry pure fruit spread instead, plus ½ tsp strong prepared mustard (or more to taste).

Brussels Sprouts and Chestnuts in Peanut Sauce

This is a rich combination of holiday specialities. For convenience, use a tin of vacuum-packed whole chestnuts.

SERVES 4–6

110–175 g/4–6 oz whole, fresh chestnuts with shells *or* 1 × 240-g/9-oz tin of cooked, shelled chestnuts
450 g/1 lb Brussels sprouts
120 ml/4 fl oz water/½ cup
50 g/2 oz/¼ cup smooth peanut butter
1½ tsp soy sauce

If you are using fresh chestnuts, first, boil them for 35–40 minutes or cook them in a pressure cooker for 15 minutes. Peel off the skins while they are still warm. Try to keep as many whole as possible.

Trim the Brussels sprouts and score the ends of the stems. Bring 5 cm/2 in water to the boil in a medium-sized saucepan, cover and steam until tender. Drain, then return them to the pan.

Meanwhile, in a small saucepan, boil the measured water and add the peanut butter, stirring until the mixture is smooth. Add the soy sauce, stir, then mix with the Brussels sprouts.

Crumble 5 or 6 chestnuts (or more if they have crumbled while peeling) and add to the saucepan with the Brussels sprouts and the peanut sauce. Stir in the remaining whole chestnuts, heat through and serve.

French Beans with Peanut Sesame Sauce

The combination of toasted sesame seeds and a creamy, peanut butter sauce brings out the taste of French or runner beans. This is delicious warm or at room temperature.

SERVES 4

4 tbsp white sesame seeds *or* unhulled ones, washed well
450 g/1 lb French *or* runner beans
110 g/4 oz/½ cup smooth peanut butter
175 ml/6 fl oz/¾ cup water

Roast the sesame seeds in a dry frying pan for a few minutes, stirring and watching that they do not burn. Remove the pan from the heat as they turn golden brown and leave to cool.

Top, tail and remove any strings from the beans and cut into 5-cm/2-in lengths. Bring 2.5 cm/1 in of water to the boil, drop in the beans, cover and cook for 2–5 minutes, or until the beans are tender, but still slightly crunchy. Lift the beans on to a plate with a slotted spoon and cover to keep warm.

Add the peanut butter to the bean cooking water in the pan, add the measured water, lower the heat and stir. Then add 3 tablespoons of the sesame seeds. Return the beans to the pan and stir to cover with the sauce. Spoon the beans and sauce on to a serving plate and sprinkle the remaining sesame seeds over.

Runner Beans in Mustard Sauce

SuperSpread makes an instant, fluffy, mayonnaise-like sauce, coupled with a mild mustard flavour.

SERVES 4–6

450 g/1 lb runner beans
4 tbsp SuperSpread
4 tbsp mild organic mustard

Top and tail the runner beans, then remove the strings running along each of the long sides. Wash, then chop them into 5-cm/2-in lengths (or leave whole if they are small, young beans).

Boil the beans, covered, in 2.5–5 cm/1–2 in of water, steaming them for 5 minutes or until they are just cooked.

Meanwhile, stir the SuperSpread and mustard together to make a light, yellow sauce.

Drain the beans and put a dollop of the sauce on each serving. Serve hot or at room temperature (if doing the latter, you should refresh the beans in cold water after cooking so they keep their colour).

Variation

This sauce goes well with other steamed vegetables; try it with cauliflower florets, broccoli and broad beans.

Kombu and Mushroom Casserole

As well as being packed full of nutrients, seaweed is also a great delicacy, with an interesting texture and sun-kissed subtle flavour.

SERVES 4–6

20 g/¾ oz dried kombu *or* wakame *or* a mixture of the two
10 g/¼ oz dried wild mushrooms *and/or* 110 g/4 oz fresh mushrooms (both optional)
1 tbsp olive oil, plus extra for greasing
1 large *or* 3 small onions
3 cloves garlic, peeled
1 × 454-g/16-oz jar Italiano or Mushroom Italiano spaghetti sauce

Soak the kombu or wakame or both in hot water for 15 minutes. If using wakame, soak it separately and do not cook it. Soak the dried mushrooms, if using, in another bowl for 15–20 minutes. Pre-cook the kombu and dried mushrooms in separate saucepans until they are tender (5–15 minutes, depending on the type of kombu). In a large jug, reserve 350 ml/12 fl oz/1½ cups of the kombu cooking water (wakame soaking water can be highly flavoured, so check and dilute it with a little plain water if this is the case).

Meanwhile, grease a shallow baking dish. Slice the onion, thickly, and spread the slices over the bottom of the dish. Pre-heat the oven to 200°C/400°F/Gas Mark 6.

Slice the garlic cloves into the opened jar of Italiano sauce and stir in the remaining olive oil. Slice the fresh mushrooms, if using.

Add the Italiano sauce mixture to the jug of reserved seaweed water and mix. Pour half this over the onions. Pour off the dried mushroom cooking liquid and save it to use in a risotto or for stock. Next, make a layer of seaweed and mushrooms over the Italiano sauce mixture, then pour the remaining Italiano sauce mixture over the top. Bake, uncovered, in the pre-heated oven for 20 minutes. Serve hot or cold.

Broccoli with Super Hollandaise

The classic hollandaise sauce is normally made with egg yolks, butter and some skill. This SuperSpread version is deliciously creamy and practically foolproof, as well as being much lower in fat and suitable for vegans and those on food-combining diets. The asafoetida gives it a hint of extra egginess and brings out the flavour of the broccoli. This is not always readily available, but, if this is the case, simply use more lemon juice and tarragon to taste.

SERVES 4

110 g/4 oz/½ cup SuperSpread
4 tbsp water
¼ tsp lemon juice
tiny pinch of asafoetida *or* a few leaves of fresh or dried tarragon
small pinch of cayenne pepper
750 g–1 kg/1½–2¼ lb broccoli, broken into small florets

First, make the sauce by putting all the ingredients, bar the broccoli, into a small saucepan and whisking them together over a medium heat until warm. Taste and add a tiny bit more lemon juice or cayenne. Asafoetida increases in taste as it sits, so only add a tiny bit more if needed. Cover and keep warm, or reheat before serving.

Meanwhile, boil some salted water, add the broccoli, then turn off the water. Leave for 6–8 minutes, when the broccoli should be tender. Remove the broccoli to a heated plate and spoon the sauce over.

DESSERTS

Banana Ice-Cream Pie with Hot Fudge Sauce

Only die-hard sugar and chocaholics will be less than satisfied with this vegan, no-added-sugar, no-chocolate treat. The ice-cream is made from frozen bananas, which turn into a soft whip when whizzed in a food processor. There are four layers altogether: a coconut peanut crust, a peanut toffee filling, then the banana ice-cream, all topped with stupendously thick hot fudge sauce.
Note that you will need to prepare and freeze the bananas at least 24 hours ahead of time.

SERVES 6

For the Banana Ice-cream
4 large *or* 6 small very ripe bananas, cut into 5-cm/2-in chunks and frozen solid (easiest done the day before)
1 tsp vanilla essence
1 tsp brown rice syrup *or* date syrup (optional)

For the crust
75 g/3 oz/1 cup desiccated *or* shredded coconut
4 tbsp/¼ cup crunchy peanut butter (salted)

For the toffee filling
3 tbsp organic brown rice syrup *or* 1½ tbsp date syrup
3 tbsp soya *or* cows' milk
50 g/2 oz/¼ cup crunchy peanut butter

For the Hot Fudge Sauce
120 ml/4 fl oz/½ cup organic brown rice syrup *or* date syrup
250 ml/8 fl oz/1 cup soya milk
50 g/2 oz/½ cup carob powder (medium *or* light-coloured)
225 g/8 oz/1 cup crunchy peanut butter
1 tsp non-hydrogenated margarine
1 tsp vanilla essence

Make the crust by dry roasting the coconut in a large frying pan or under the grill until it is golden-flecked, watching it carefully as it burns easily. Some of it will still be white. Stir the peanut butter into the hot coconut and mix together until melted. Press this mixture against the sides of an 18-cm/7-in non-metallic pie dish and leave to cool.

Next, put all the toffee filling ingredients into a saucepan. Stir them together quickly over a medium heat for 1 minute until combined and then immediately spread the mixture over the flat bottom of the pie dish only. Leave it to cool. These 2 steps for the pie crust can be done in advance and the pie frozen, if you wish.

Whizz the frozen bananas with the vanilla in a food processor until as smooth as ice-cream. Taste and add 1 teaspoon or more of brown rice syrup or date syrup if needed. Pile it into the prepared crust and keep it in the freezer until you want to serve it, as it melts very quickly after whizzing. This can be done well in advance (in which case transfer it to the fridge for 30 minutes before serving), but the texture of the ice-cream is nicest when freshly done.

For the Hot Fudge Sauce, put all the sauce ingredients into a saucepan (this can be done well before the meal), then, just before serving, combine them quickly over a medium heat. It will get hot and thick within minutes, after which it burns easily, so remove it from the heat as soon as it is ready.

Cut the pie and serve with a large dollop of the Hot Fudge Sauce on each. Keep the remaining sauce warm in the oven or over a candle or reheat it quickly for second helpings.

Cherry Ice-Cream

This is a soft ice-cream with a full-bodied cherry flavour. It also works well as the basis of a cherry ice-cream soda. Put two scoops into a tall glass and top up with no-added-sugar cola. This is the first of three recipes that uses an egg white substitute made from linseeds, which gives the ice-cream its scoopable texture.

SERVES 4–6
1 tbsp whole linseeds (flax seeds)
250 ml/8 fl oz/1 cup water
2 × 283-g/10-oz jars cherry pure fruit spread
600 ml/1 pint/1⅛ cups soya milk
120 ml/4 fl oz/½ cup apple juice concentrate
2 tsp vanilla essence

First, boil the linseeds in the water in a small uncovered saucepan for 2 minutes. Put the seeds and liquid into a food processor and whizz for 30 seconds. Sieve, throw away the seeds in the sieve. Parts of some of the linseeds may slip through but it does not matter. What remains is the 'linseed white'. Cool, then chill it in the fridge for 15 minutes.

Then, measure 2 tablespoons of the linseed white into the food processor (the rest will keep for up to two weeks and is an excellent egg substitute — 4 tablespoons replaces 1 egg — or use it in Two Ice-Creams That Go Like a Bombe on page 104 or Peanut Butter Cookies on page 122).

Remove the whole cherries from the cherry spread and reserve them in the fridge. Mix the remaining cherry spread, soya milk, apple juice concentrate and vanilla essence with the measured linseed white. Freeze for 2 hours in a shallow, freezerproof container. Break up the crystals that have formed with a fork or in the food processor. Fold in the reserved cherries and freeze again. Defrost for 15 minutes before serving.

Variation
For strawberry ice-cream, simply use strawberry pure fruit spread instead of the cherry.

Peanut Butter and Blueberry Ice-Cream

This is the classic American combination of peanut butter and jam turned into a creamy ice-cream. It has proved highly popular with adults because of its unusually soft texture and the contrasting flavours.

SERVES 6

150 ml/5 fl oz/⅝ cup apple juice concentrate
1 × 312-g/11-oz jar *or* 1¼ cups smooth, unsalted peanut butter
475 ml/16 fl oz/2 cups soya milk (cows' milk does not work well)
215 g/7½ oz/¾ cup/jar blueberry pure fruit spread

Put the apple juice concentrate into a food processor or liquidizer. Add the peanut butter and milk and whizz until smooth. Pour the ice-cream into a shallow, freezerproof container and freeze for 2½ hours, or until nearly solid. Alternatively, pour it into smaller individual containers and freeze for 1½–2 hours.

Swirl the blueberry pure fruit spread through the partially frozen ice-cream and freeze again until solid (about 6 hours). This ice-cream can be scooped directly from the freezer, but it will be creamier if it is removed from the freezer 30 minutes before serving.

Two Ice-Creams That Go Like a Bombe

Light almond and dark carob ice-creams can be packed into a bombe mould and served with the Hot Fudge Sauce for a special dessert. This ice-cream needs to be beaten or whizzed just before serving to avoid crystals forming. However, the sauce can be made in advance and reheated.

SERVES 6

For the Ice-creams
**1 tbsp whole linseeds (flax seeds) (see Cherry Ice-Cream)
250 ml/8 fl oz/1 cup water
75 g/3 oz creamed coconut
475 ml/16 fl oz/2 cups soya milk
120 ml/4 fl oz/½ cup brown rice syrup
2 tsp vanilla essence
2 tbsp medium roast carob powder
25 g/1 oz/¼ cup toasted blanched almonds, plus an optional 25 g/1 oz/¼ cup**

For the Hot Fudge Sauce
**4 tbsp carob powder
1 tbsp cornflour
250 ml/8 fl oz/1 cup soya milk
5 tbsp brown rice syrup
1 tsp vanilla essence
50 g/2 oz/4 tbsp unsalted butter *or* non-hydrogenated margarine**

Put the linseeds into a small saucepan with the water. Bring to the boil, uncovered, then boil for 2 minutes until the mixture has reduced slightly. Pour into a food processor and whizz for 30 seconds to partially crush the seeds. Sieve. Measure 120 ml/4 fl oz/½ cup of the liquid and refrigerate for 15 minutes (keep any extra for another recipe).

Melt the creamed coconut over a low heat with 4 tablespoons of water.

Mix the refrigerated linseed white with the soya milk, brown rice syrup, melted creamed coconut and vanilla and whizz in the food processor. Pour this mixture into a measuring jug and return exactly half of it to the food processor. Add the carob powder to this and whizz. Pour the plain and carob mixtures into separate, shallow freezerproof containers and freeze solid.

About an hour before serving, whizz the plain ice-cream in the food processor, then stir in 25 g/1 oz/¼ cup of the toasted almonds. If making a bombe, pack what is now the almond ice-cream into a 1.2-litre/2-pint bombe mould. Put a small bowl in the centre to make an impression, then remove it and smooth the surface. Now whizz the carob ice-cream and add the remaining toasted almonds, if using. Pack the ice-cream into the mould. Return the bombe to the freezer until ready to serve.

Make the Hot Fudge Sauce just a few minutes before serving by sieving the carob and cornflour into a saucepan. Turn on the heat and whisk in the soya milk, a bit at a time, until a smooth paste is formed. Add the brown rice syrup and continue whisking until fluffy. Turn off the heat and whisk in the vanilla and butter or margarine.

Turn the bombe out on to a plate (if necessary, warm the outside of the mould briefly in hot water, to help loosen it). Serve the sauce hot over the bombe or on one or other of the ice-creams if serving them separately.

Variation: Iced Coffee

Make 1 cup of coffee, decaffeinated if preferred, per person and leave to cool. Put 2 scoops of either the toasted almond or carob ice-cream in the bottom of a tall glass and pour the coffee over it. It is not absolutely necessary to have whizzed the frozen ice-cream for this.

Or Make each person a cup of Wake Cup, using 2 teaspoons of the powder in each cup, and pour this over the toasted almond ice-cream in a tall glass (the carob ice-cream and Wake Cup do not mix well).

Strawberry and Almond Ice-Cream

Here is a way to have delicious organic strawberry ice-cream all year round.

SERVES 4

275 ml/9 fl oz/1⅛ cups soya milk
225 ml/7 fl oz/⅞ cup water
1 tsp agar agar powder *or* 1 tbsp agar agar flakes
2 × 283-g/10-oz jars strawberry pure fruit spread
½ tsp vanilla essence
1 tsp fresh lemon juice
up to 50 g/2 oz/⅓ cup whole, blanched almonds (optional)

Put the soya milk, water, agar agar, half the strawberry spread and the vanilla into a saucepan. Heat it to boiling point, whisking in the pure fruit spread and making sure that the agar agar has dissolved (if you have used flakes). Then, leave it to cool.

Once the ice-cream mixture has cooled, pour it into a shallow freezerproof container and freeze for 2 hours.

Then, beat it by hand to break up the crystals or do this in a food processor — note that if a food processor is used the ice-cream can be frozen much longer, until just before serving, otherwise, remove it from the freezer 30 minutes before serving. Break up the remaining strawberry spread, mix in the lemon juice, then stir this into the ice-cream sufficiently to give a marbled pattern. Alternatively, pulse it in a food processor. Fold in the almonds, if using, then return the ice-cream to the freezer for an hour. This ice-cream is best freshly made as crystals will form again and the almonds will soften.

Pineapple Sorbet with Cherries

This is a creamy, rather than icy sorbet that can be scooped straight from the freezer. When milk powder is used, it is an even creamier, low-fat ice-cream. The cherries are optional, but truly delicious.

Serves 4–6

40 g/1½ oz/¾ cup soya milk powder *or* 50 g/2 oz/¾ cup cows' milk powder
175 ml/6 fl oz/¾ cup water
scant ½ tsp almond essence
2 × 283-g/10-oz jars pineapple pure fruit spread
150 g/5 oz/½ cup/½ jar cherry pure fruit spread (optional)

This can be made in a bowl, a food processor or a liquidizer. Dissolve the milk powder in the water and add the almond essence (measure it carefully as it is quite a strong flavour).

Mix the pineapple spread in the jars, then stir it into the milk mixture. Pour this into a shallow freezerproof container, then swirl in the cherry spread, just enough to marble the pineapple mixture. Freeze for 2 hours, or until needed.

Blackcurrant Sorbet

This is a pure fruit sorbet with a clear blackcurrant flavour. Kiwi and Golden Plum also work well, but the blackcurrant version is really special.

SERVES 4

**150 ml/5 fl oz/⅝ cup apple juice concentrate
350 ml/12 fl oz/1½ cups water
5 tsp arrowroot
1 × 283-g/10-oz jar blackcurrant pure fruit spread
4 sprigs of fresh mint, plus extra to garnish (optional) *or* julienne strips of lime zest, to decorate**

In a saucepan, whisk together the apple juice concentrate with the water and arrowroot. Bring to the boil, stirring, then reduce the heat a bit and stir frequently until the mixture has thickened slightly (about 5 minutes).

Leave it to cool for 5 minutes or so, stirring to release the steam once or twice. Whisk in the blackcurrant spread until well mixed.

Pour the ice-cream into a shallow freezerproof container, chop and stir in the mint leaves, if using, then freeze for 2–3 hours. Remove it to the fridge 30 minutes before serving and decorate the portions with the extra mint leaves, if using, or the julienne strips of lime.

Peach Melba Granita

Peach Melba pure fruit spread makes a two-flavour granita, because of the solid pieces of peach amidst the raspberry ice shavings. Blackcurrant or blueberry pure fruit spread decorated with mint are also delicious, but experiment trying any of your favourite flavours.

SERVES 3–4

**1 × 283-g/10-oz jar Peach Melba pure fruit spread
250 ml/8 fl oz/1 cup water
3–4 sprigs of fresh mint, to decorate (optional)**

In a shallow, freezerproof container, stir the pure fruit spread and water together, breaking up any lumps. Freeze until the mixture has set solid (2½–4 hours minimum).

Just before serving, fork through the granita until you have icy shavings. Spoon it into 3 or 4 goblets. Add a sprig of mint to decorate.

Raspberry and Apricot Frozen Yogurt Parfaits

The ingredients for these desserts are simple and relatively low in calories, yet these parfaits are wonderfully sumptuous. A single-flavour parfait could be made, using one fruit and twice as much yogurt.

Serves 4

1½ tsp brown rice syrup
1½ tsp vanilla essence
400 g/14 oz/1½ cups soya *or* cows' milk yogurt
1 × 283-g/10-oz jar raspberry pure fruit spread
1 × 283-g/10-oz jar apricot pure fruit spread
2–3 tbsp shelled, unsalted pistachios, lightly toasted

Mix the brown rice syrup and vanilla into the yogurt, taste and add more syrup if it is still acidic. Divide it equally among 3 bowls.

Add 6 tablespoons of the raspberry spread to one bowl and the same amount of apricot spread to another bowl and mix each well.

Divide the raspberry yogurt between 4 small glass goblets. Then, carefully, put half of the vanilla yogurt on top. Spoon all of the apricot yogurt on top, then the remaining vanilla yogurt. Stir the remaining jam in the jars to break it up. Put a dollop of each in the middle of the top layer of yogurt and press them down through the layers. Press the pistachios through the layers in the same way and put the goblets into the freezer. They will be ready to serve after 30 minutes or so, when the parfaits will be thick and cold. You can freeze them for a longer time, but it will then be necessary to defrost them at room temperature for 15–30 minutes before serving.

Fruity Fools

This is a special treat that can be made in an instant. A thick, tinned coconut milk is needed; home-made ones are too thin. Try Dunn's River, Jedi or Thai brands from West Indian, Oriental, Indian and some health food shops.

Serves 4

1 × 400-ml/14-fl oz tin *or* 1¼ cups coconut milk
425 g/15 oz/1½ cups apricot *or* raspberry *or* pineapple *or* Peach Melba pure fruit spread

First, beat the coconut milk well by hand, in a food processor or liquidizer. Add the fruit spread of your choice and mix it in very well (try to leave the pieces of peach whole if you are using Peach Melba). Pour the fool mixture into 4 small goblets and chill until you are ready to serve (but for at least 30 minutes).

Rose Berries

The rose petals add a subtle flavour to this mixture of gooseberries, blackcurrants, raspberries and blackberries, but this 'cream' is just as delicious (and pink) without them.
You can use those petals on the verge of falling to avoid destroying the whole flower, although they will brown faster. Gently wash and pat them dry with kitchen paper, and store them in a closed plastic bag in the fridge if you will not be using them immediately.

Serves 4

120 g/4½ oz/1 cup pine nuts
1 × 283-g/10-oz jar Mixed Berry pure fruit spread
6 tbsp soya milk
a large handful of rose petals from unsprayed flowers (optional)
1 kiwi fruit, peeled and sliced (optional)

Grind the pine nuts to a smooth paste in a food processor, an electric coffee grinder or mortar and pestle.

Mix the pine nut paste with Mixed Berry fruit spread and soya milk until well combined.

Decorate small bowls or goblets with some of the rose petals, if using. Add the berry cream and put a few more petals on top to decorate. Alternatively, put two slices of kiwi fruit on top of each portion. Chill, if not serving immediately.

Sweet Lemon and Avocado Cream

For the best results, make this treat just before serving. Avocados vary in size and taste and some organic ones are so delicious and delicate that you will need a much smaller amount of Lemon Shred.

Serves 4

4 small avocados
up to 425 g/15 oz/1½ jars Lemon Shred
2 tsp flaked almonds
1 tsp fresh mint, chopped (optional)

Peel the avocados and remove the stones, then mash the flesh in a food processor or a bowl. Mix in three quarters of the Lemon Shred, taste and add more if needed.

Spoon the mixture into small goblets, sprinkle with the flaked almonds and scatter the mint, if using, on top. Keep in the fridge if not serving within 30 minutes.

Per person:
1 small avocado
up to 100 g/3½ oz/⅜ cup Lemon Shred
a few flaked almonds
sprigs of mint, optional

Meglie-Lebanese Festive Pudding

This aromatic and beguiling sweet is adapted from a Lebanese recipe, traditionally served when a child is born. Although 'meglie' translates as 'milk pudding', there is no milk in the original recipe. Its smooth texture and subtle flavour are complemented by very fresh nuts on top (if necessary, roast them in a dry frying pan or under the grill, to freshen them up).

SERVES 4

50 g/2 oz/½ cup brown rice flour
900 ml/1½ pints/3½ cups water
120 ml/4 fl oz/½ cup organic brown rice syrup, plus extra, to taste
scant ½ tsp aniseed
scant ½ tsp caraway seeds
scant ½ tsp fennel seeds
pinch of ground ginger
15 g/½ oz/2 tbsp almonds, chopped
15 g/½ oz/2 tbsp pistachios, chopped
15 g/½ oz/2 tbsp walnuts, chopped

In a medium-sized bowl, combine the brown rice flour and 4 tablespoons of the water. Gradually stir in a further 8 tablespoons until a smooth paste is formed. Add the brown rice syrup and spices and mix.

Bring 600 ml/1 pint/2½ cups of the water to the boil. Add the brown rice flour mixture, gradually, stirring constantly to prevent lumps forming. Bring to the boil, then reduce the heat to low, cover and simmer, stirring occasionally, for 10 minutes. It should then be thick enough to coat the back of a spoon.

Let it cool slightly, then pour it into 4 bowls. Leave it to cool completely, then chill until ready to serve, then, sprinkle with the chopped nuts and, possibly, more brown rice syrup to taste.

Quick Fruit Pudding

It takes less than five minutes to gather all the ingredients together and start cooking this pudding, and it can be varied to suit your needs. Try it at whatever oven temperature you are cooking your main course at, and bake it for up to an hour if you are not ready for the pudding straight away. The measures are just a guideline; essentially it is fruit, pure fruit spread and muesli on top, dotted with margarine and cinnamon. The cereal absorbs the pure fruit spread and makes a wonderful fruit sauce.

Serves 4–6

2 tbsp non-hydrogenated margarine *or* SuperSpread
3–4 pears *or* apples
1 × 283-g/10-oz/1 cup pure fruit spread (any type — except marmalade — *or* a mixture of types)
½ tsp ground cinnamon
90–165 g/3½–5½ oz/½ cup **Almond Crunch** *or* muesli or granola-type cereal
soya milk *or* cream, to serve

Pre-heat the oven to 180°C/350°F/Gas Mark 4.

Grease a baking dish (about 25 cm/10 in across with some of the margarine or SuperSpread. Slice the fruit thinly and distribute it over the base of the dish.

Break up the fruit spread in the jar and spread it over the fruit. Dust over the cinnamon.

Spread the cereal over the top. Dot the remaining margarine or SuperSpread over the top (if using SuperSpread, stir it into the Almond Crunch or muesli).

Bake the pudding for 15–30 minutes, depending on the fruit (apples take longer than pears). Serve warm with soya milk or cream.

Baked Apples Three Ways

Depending on what you have in the cupboard — cookers, dessert apples, pure fruit spread, or syrup — one of these recipes should appeal. The first two are also good at room temperature, served with yogurt.

SERVES 4

4 medium cooking apples
2 tsp Super Spread *or* non-hydrogenated margarine *or* butter, plus extra ½ tsp (optional)
4 tbsp strawberry *or* raspberry pure fruit spread, plus extra 4 tbsp (optional)
25 g/1 oz/4 tbsp ground almonds

Pre-heat the oven to 200°C/400°F/Gas Mark 6. Wash, then core the apples to within 1 cm/½ in of the bottom, making a 2.5-cm/1-in diameter hole. Spread some of the SuperSpread, margarine or butter in the hole of each apple.

Mix the strawberry or raspberry spread and ground almonds together and stuff into the holes in the apples.

Place the apples in a roasting tin. Boil 120 ml/4 fl oz/½ cup of water and pour it into the pan around the apples. Bake them in the pre-heated oven for 30 minutes or until tender.

For a warm sauce, remove the apples from the tin once they are done, add 4 tablespoons of strawberry or raspberry spread and ½ teaspoon of margarine or butter to the juices and, over heat, stir until thickened.

Variations

Use a dessert apple and Hedgerow pure fruit spread, the ground almonds and 1 teaspoon of ground cinnamon mixed together to fill the apples.

Or use dessert instead of cooking apples and peel, core and slice them thickly, horizontally. Spread the following mixture on each slice: 4 tablespoons SuperSpread, margarine or butter, 1 tablespoon organic brown rice syrup, 1 tablespoon chopped walnuts and 1 teaspoon ground cinnamon. Reassemble the apples and bake them on a greased baking tray in the oven pre-heated to 180°C/350°F/Gas Mark 4 for 30 minutes.

Quick Rice Pudding

Serves 2–3

1 × 440-g/15½-oz tin *or* 3 cups Organic Ready Rice
250 ml/8 fl oz/1 cup soya milk
2 tsp arrowroot
3–4 tbsp organic brown rice syrup *or* maize syrup to taste

Optional flavourings
3 tbsp sultanas *or* raisins
or 4–6 cardamom pods, broken
or strawberry *or* other pure fruit spread
and/or toasted cashews
and/or a sprinkling of ground cinnamon

After removing the rice from the tin and breaking it up, steam it over water; this makes the rice really soft.

Mix the soya milk and arrowroot together. Drain off the steaming water and tip the rice into the pan. Add the soya milk mixture, syrup and sultanas or raisins or cardamom pods, if using. Bring to the boil, then simmer, uncovered, until it has thickened (about 3 minutes), stirring occasionally to prevent it sticking.

Spoon the pudding into 2 or 3 bowls and top with the strawberry or other fruit spread and/or nuts and/or cinnamon.

Variation
This baked version is soft inside and crisped on top.

1 × 440-g/15½-oz tin/3 cups Organic Ready Rice
325 ml/11 fl oz/1⅓ cups soya milk
2½ tbsp barley malt *or* maize *or* organic brown rice syrup
1 tsp vanilla essence
3–4 tbsp sultanas *or* raisins
½ tsp ground cinnamon (optional)
½ tsp grated lemon zest (optional)

Pre-heat the oven to 180°C/350°F/Gas Mark 4.

In a greased, ovenproof casserole, empty the tin of rice and fork through. Pour over the remaining ingredients and mix well. Bake, covered, in the pre-heated oven for 40 minutes, uncover it, then return to the oven to bake for 10 minutes more, to brown the top.

Bread and Butter Pudding

There are so many types of brown bread — from those that are really no more than white bread with artificial colouring (and sugar and preservatives), to sourdough organic rye. There are those who say that a non-organic wholemeal loaf is so loaded with pesticides that it would be better to eat white bread. This idea is based on the fact that the spray remains in the outer layers of the whole grain and is then baked in. The answer is to buy organic bread (and wholemeal pasta, oats and other grains) where possible.

For this recipe a yeasted wheat bread works best. Because breads vary in density, the weight is just a guideline; cut enough to make two layers in the size of baking dish you will be using.

SERVES 4

475 ml/16 fl oz/2 cups soya milk
2½ tsp arrowroot
1 vanilla pod *or* 2 tsp vanilla essence
5 tbsp brown rice syrup
approximately 350 g/12 oz fresh, light wholemeal bread
3 tbsp SuperSpread *or* non-hydrogenated margarine *or* butter
25 g/1 oz/¼ cup sultanas

For topping
ground cinnamon, to taste (optional)
3 tbsp apricot pure fruit spread
2 tbsp brown rice syrup

Pre-heat the oven to 180°C/350°F/Gas Mark 4. Grease a 23–25-cm/9–10-in baking dish or 2 smaller ones.

In a saucepan, whisk together the soya milk and arrowroot. Heat it, with the vanilla pod, if using, until slightly thickened. Whisk in the brown rice syrup and add the vanilla essence if you are using this instead of the vanilla pod.

Meanwhile, cut the crusts off the bread and slice it fairly thinly. Spread both sides with SuperSpread or margarine or butter. Arrange the slices in the prepared baking dish, or dishes, making 2 even layers, scattering the sultanas between them.

Pour most of the soya milk mixture over the bread, allowing time for the bread to absorb it, then add more if the bread can absorb it. There should not be any pools of milk — either pour these off or add some more bread. Bake, uncovered, in the pre-heated oven for 30 minutes, or until the top has browned slightly.

To make the topping, sprinkle over a little cinnamon, if liked, then mix the apricot spread with the syrup and spread it in a thin layer over the top of the pudding. Grill until the topping is bubbly, then serve.

Hot Pineapple with Lemon Shred and Ginger

Warm pineapple, which contains the digestive enzyme bromelain, and ginger, noted for its settling qualities, combine to make a delicious, naturally sweet, light pudding. It is also very good cold, served in its jelly.

Serves 4

1 large, very ripe, pineapple (pull one of the leaves: if it comes off easily, the pineapple is ready)
350 ml/12 fl oz/1 ½ cups water
2.5-cm/1-in piece fresh root ginger, peeled and thinly sliced
185 g/6½ oz/⅔ cup Lemon Shred

With a sharp knife, cut the top off the pineapple, then slice off the skin. Cut it into 5-mm/¼-in thick slices, then cut out the core (this can be done in advance and the pineapple covered and kept in the fridge).

Put the water, ginger and Lemon Shred into a large saucepan, bring to the boil and simmer for 1 minute. Add the sliced pineapple, reduce the heat and simmer for 7 minutes. Serve hot, on warmed plates, pouring the extra sauce over.

Sladké Knedlíky (Czech Sweet Dumplings)

On a visit to Prague, I ordered dumplings in a cafeteria, expecting something heavy and savoury. Instead, what arrived was a delicious, raised, sweet dumpling, doused in butter and cinnamon and filled with plum jam. The following recipe closely resembles the treat I had that day, although it is quite different to the traditional recipe, which would be yeasted and simmered in muslin packages. This is a very filling and substantial sweet.

MAKES 8 LARGE DUMPLINGS

4 tbsp poppy seeds
6 tbsp brown rice syrup
2 tbsp water
oil, for greasing
225 g/8 oz/2 cups self-raising wholemeal flour
½ tsp sea salt
3–4 tbsp blueberry *or* Hedgerow pure fruit spread
110 g/4 oz/½ cup salted butter *or* non-hydrogenated margarine
ground cinnamon, for dusting

Dry roast the poppy seeds in a frying pan until they are sweet-smelling, but no longer as they burn easily.

Heat the brown rice syrup and water together, then leave to cool.

Warm 4 plates and grease a steamer basket well with oil. Bring 5–8 cm/2–3 in of water to the boil to use with the steamer in a large, wide saucepan.

Meanwhile, sieve the flour and salt into a bowl. Pour in the syrup and water mixture and stir until well mixed. Knead for a minute or two, sprinkling in a little more flour if the dough is too sticky. Divide the dough into 8 equal pieces and either roll it out or pat it flat to form a circle about 10 cm/4 in in diameter. Put 1½–2 teaspoons of the blueberry or Hedgerow spread in the centre, then bring the edges together and twist to form a round, sealed package. Work quickly, doing the same to make the other 7 dumplings, then steam, covered, for 7 minutes.

Then, melt half the butter or margarine in a large frying pan.

When it is sizzling turn the dumplings in it, briefly, on all sides until they are golden brown. Put 2 dumplings on each plate, quickly melt the remaining butter and pour it over the dumplings. Sprinkle the cinnamon and poppy seeds over and serve warm.

Marmalade and Hot Fudge Crêpe Gâteaux

Carob crêpes are here layered with warm marmalade and coconut, then served with Hot Fudge Sauce for a sumptuous winter pudding. This will make four, four-layered servings or sixteen single crêpes.
Note that the crêpe batter needs to be chilled for 30 minutes before using.

Serves 4–8

For the crêpes
120 g/4½ oz/1 cup wholemeal flour *or* brown rice flour
25 g/1 oz/½ cup soya flour
3 tbsp medium roast carob flour
pinch of sea salt
1 tsp baking powder
1 tsp cinnamon
2 tbsp barley malt
1 tsp vanilla essence
325 ml/11 fl oz/1⅓ cups water
oil, for frying

For the Hot Fudge Sauce
6 tbsp carob powder
1 tbsp cornflour
250 ml/8 fl oz/1 cup soya *or* cows' milk
4 tbsp apple juice concentrate
50 g/2 oz/4 tbsp unsalted butter *or* non-hydrogenated margarine
1 tsp vanilla essence

For assembling gâteaux
50 g/2 oz/¾ cup desiccated coconut
1 × 283-g/10-oz jar Orange Shred (sweet 'n' fruity)

First, make the crêpes by mixing all crêpes ingredients, except the oil, together in a food processor. If mixing by hand, sieve the flours into a bowl with the salt, baking powder and cinnamon. Add the barley malt and vanilla, then, gradually, the water and beat it well. If the mixture is very thick, add up to 2 tablespoons of water to make a thin cream. Chill the batter for 30 minutes.

Meanwhile, prepare the Hot Fudge Sauce. Sieve the carob and cornflour into a saucepan. Add the milk slowly, stirring until the mixture is smooth. Stir in the apple juice concentrate. Turn on the heat to medium, add the butter or margarine and stir constantly until a smooth, thick sauce is produced. Take off the heat and whisk in the vanilla. Keep it covered and reheat just before serving.

Turn the oven on to a low heat to warm some plates and keep the crêpes warm as they are made. Have ready the desiccated coconut, the opened jar of Orange Shred and a spoon. If you have them, use two or three good frying or crêpe pans to make the crêpes quickly. Heat a pan and oil it lightly. The pan is ready for frying if a drop of crêpe mixture sizzles. Reduce the heat to medium, then add 2 tablespoons of mixture to the pan, immediately smoothing it out to a thin, even layer with the back of the spoon. Cook until bubbles begin to show over the top. Flip the crêpe over and, while the other side is cooking, gently spread 1 tablespoon of Orange Shred over the centre (this warms the marmalade through). When the other side has cooked, remove the crêpe to a baking tray, sprinkle some coconut on top and keep warm in the oven, covered with foil. Repeat until all the batter, Orange Shred and coconut have been used up.

Pile 4 crêpes on top of each other, spoon Hot Fudge Sauce on top and serve 1 crêpe gâteau to each person. Alternatively, each crêpe can be rolled after making, serving 2 per person with sauce.

BISCUITS, SWEETS, CAKES AND OTHER TREATS

Ginger Nuts

A crunchy biscuit with a gingery, peppery taste, these are similar to the commercially available ginger nuts, but made from wholesome ingredients.

Makes 24–28

290 g/10½ oz/1¾ cups wholemeal flour
½ tsp ground cinnamon
250 g/9 oz/¾ cup brown rice syrup
2 tbsp oil, plus extra for greasing
1½ tsp grated fresh ginger root
½ tsp bicarbonate of soda dissolved in 1 tsp water

Pre-heat the oven to 190°C/375°F/Gas Mark 5.

Mix all the ingredients together well. Roll the dough out on a well-floured board to a thickness of 5 mm/¼ in. Cut out small rounds, and bake in the pre-heated oven on a greased baking tray in batches for 10–12 minutes. Remove them quickly to a wire cooling rack where they will immediately harden. Store the Ginger Nuts in an airtight container and eat within a week.

Peanut Butter Cookies

Peanut butter cookies are an American classic, usually made with granulated sugar and eggs. This recipe makes an irresistible cookie, very close to the crispy and chewy original, with no eggs or sugar.

MAKES 30–36

1 tbsp whole linseeds (flax seeds)
250 ml/8 fl oz/1 cup water
225 g/8 oz/1 cup crunchy peanut butter
50 ml/2 fl oz/¼ cup vegetable oil, plus extra for greasing
250 g/9 oz/¾ cup brown rice syrup
2 tsp vanilla essence
75 g/3 oz/¾ cup wholemeal flour
40 g/1½ oz/¼ cup wholemeal semolina or ground almonds (for a granulated texture)

First, make the egg substitute by putting the linseeds into a small saucepan with the water. Bring to the boil then boil, uncovered, for 2 minutes, until the mixture has reduced slightly. Pour into a food processor and whizz for about 30 seconds to partially crush the seeds. Sieve. Parts of some of the seeds may slip through, but it does not matter. Refrigerate the linseed white for 15 minutes while measuring the rest of the ingredients.

Pre-heat the oven to 190°C/375°F/Gas Mark 5.

In a food processor or large bowl, combine the peanut butter, oil, brown rice syrup and vanilla. Add the flour and semolina or ground almonds and mix. Then, add 4 tablespoons of the linseed white and mix (save the rest for Cherry Ice-Cream or Two Ice-Creams That Go Like a Bombe on pages 102 and 104 or use 4 tablespoons to replace 1 egg in other recipes; it will keep fresh in the fridge for 2 weeks or can be frozen).

Grease 2 baking trays. If a chewy cookie is preferred, drop the batter by tablespoonfuls on to the trays and spread slightly with a wetted knife to a thickness of 5 mm/¼ in. For a very thin, crispy cookie, with a less pronounced peanut flavour, drop by teaspoonfuls and flatten to a thickness of 3 mm/⅛ in. Space the cookies well, as they spread during cooking. Bake in the pre-heated oven for 13–18 minutes, or until just lightly golden, but do not allow them to brown at all or they will be overdone. Lift them with a fish slice on to a wire rack to cool before eating. Store the cookies in an airtight container and eat within a week.

Coconut Macaroons

These macaroons are moist on the inside and lightly crunchy on the outside. The brown rice syrup heightens the flavour of the coconut, as well as adding sweetness. The Lemon Macaroons of the variation are less sweet and crisp, but more delicate and soft.

Makes 13–15

1 tbsp soya *or* cows' milk
175 g/6 oz/2 cups desiccated coconut
5 tbsp organic brown rice syrup
oil, for greasing

Pre-heat the oven to 180°C/350°F/Gas Mark 4. Grease a large baking tray with a little oil.

In a medium-sized bowl, sprinkle the milk on to the coconut and mix well. Add the brown rice syrup and mix to distribute it evenly.

Roll the mixture into golf ball-sized balls with your hands and place them on the baking tray.

Bake the macaroons in the pre-heated oven for 12–15 minutes until just golden brown. Remove them to a wire cooling rack immediately. Store in an airtight container and eat within a week.

Variation: Lemon Macaroons
For these, use 150 g/5 oz/½ cup Lemon Shred instead of brown rice syrup and flatten the balls into 5-cm/2-in diameter discs before baking until lightly golden. Store these in the fridge and bring to room temperature before eating.

St Clement's Biscuits

Oranges, lemons and almonds make these light macaroon biscuits. Using a food processor will reduce the preparation time to just ten minutes, but this recipe can easily be made by hand and will not take very much longer.

Makes 15–18

4 tbsp non-hydrogenated margarine
oil, for greasing
2 small, unwaxed oranges
50 g/2 oz/½ cup whole or chopped almonds or 75 g/3 oz/⅔ cup flaked almonds
50 g/2 oz/½ cup wholemeal flour
150 g/5 oz/½ cup Lemon Shred
3 tbsp organic brown rice syrup
pinch of sea salt
½ tsp vanilla essence

Melt the margarine in a saucepan and set aside to cool.

Pre-heat the oven to 180°C/350°F/Gas Mark 4 and grease a baking tray.

Wash, dry then peel the oranges, leaving most of the pith. Bring the orange peel to the boil in sufficient water to cover, then pour the water out. Repeat this process 4 more times. This removes any bitterness. Then put the peel into a food processor and whizz until the pieces are about 5 mm/¼ in in size, or chop finely by hand.

Add the almonds and whizz until chopped, if necessary. If already chopped or flaked, just add in.

Now add the flour, Lemon Shred, brown rice syrup, salt, vanilla and melted margarine and pulse until mixed or, if making by hand, mix well together.

Drop the mixture by tablespoonfuls on to a greased baking tray. Flatten the mixture slightly with the back of a spoon to form rounds about 6 cm/2½ in in diameter. Bake in the pre-heated oven for 15–20 minutes, until the edges are golden brown. Leave to cool briefly on the baking tray, then lift them on to a wire rack to finish cooling.

Store them in the refrigerator and bring to room temperature before eating.

Three Nut Butter Truffles

This is a virtually instant confection with a delicate flavour that is full of protein due to the combination of nuts and oats. Organic brown rice syrup makes the truffles very sweet, usually preferred by people used to sugar, but the organic maize syrup gives a rounded, mellow flavour that perfectly complements the Three Nut Butter.

Makes 15–20

135 g/4¾ oz/½ cup Three Nut Butter
4 tbsp organic brown rice syrup *or* organic maize syrup
110 g/4 oz/⅞ cup fine oatmeal *or* 110 g/4 oz/1 cup rolled oats, ground in a food processor
1½ tbsp water
65 g/2½ oz/½ cup sultanas
2 tsp vanilla essence
25 g/1 oz/¼ cup desiccated coconut

Put the Three Nut Butter, syrup and oatmeal into a bowl or food processor and mix.

Add the water (measuring it very carefully), sultanas and vanilla and mix again.

Shape the mixture into balls about 2.5 cm/1 in in diameter and roll them in the coconut. Press them into a pie dish and sprinkle the remaining coconut on top. Store these in the refrigerator.

Peanut Butter Fudge

For peanut butter addicts, this is irresistible. Each little cube is a rich, sweet, soft, peanutty mouthful, and there is an optional chocolate topping. There is no dairy-free, no-added-sugar carob bar made without hydrogenated fat available at the moment. However, Green & Black's wonderful chocolate, made with 70 per cent organic cocoa, has a relatively mild effect on the blood sugar, lower even than carob, which is nature's richest source of sucrose. Alternatively, try a no-added-sugar carob spread for a very soft topping.

MAKES 16–20 PIECES

45 g/1¾ oz/½ cup rolled oats *or* scant ½ cup fine oatmeal
110 g/4 oz/½ cup American Style Peanut Butter
75 g/3 oz/⅓ cup organic brown rice syrup
1½ tsp lemon juice
carob *or* chocolate bar *or* carob spread (optional)

If using rolled oats, grind them in a clean coffee grinder or food processor. Mix them with the peanut butter, brown rice syrup and lemon juice in a bowl or whizz in a food processor.

Spread the fudge in a non-metallic 18–20-cm/7–8-in dish to a thickness of about 2.5 cm/1 in.

If using, melt your choice of carob or chocolate bar in a double boiler over hot, but not boiling, water and spread this over the top of the fudge. Leave to cool, then keep in the fridge or freezer. Cut it into small pieces and serve in paper cases.

Turkish-Style Helvah

Rich and delicious, this golden yellow helvah (the Turkish pronunciation) is a mixture of warm, ground nuts, butter, rosewater and earthy spices, instead of the rather better-known, ground, pressed, sesame seed halva. This recipe can be doubled and refrigerated for several days, but bring to room temperature before serving.

Makes 8

75 g/3 oz/⅓ cup butter *or* non-hydrogenated margarine
40 g/1½ oz/½ cup ground rolled oats, ground in a food processor, *or* oatmeal
40 g/1½ oz/½ cup ground almonds
50 g/2 oz/6 tbsp white sesame seeds
150 g/5 oz/½ cup apricot pure fruit spread
25 g/1 oz/2½ tbsp walnuts, chopped
1 tbsp rosewater
1 tsp turmeric
½ tsp ground cardamom
1–2 tsp brown rice syrup, to taste (optional)

Melt two-thirds of the butter or margarine in a frying pan. Add the oats or oatmeal, ground almonds and sesame seeds and stir for 10–12 minutes over a very low heat until the flour and seeds are pale yellow. Remove the pan from the heat

Add the apricot spread and the remaining butter or margarine to another saucepan and heat to melt them together, stirring to break up the apricot spread. Pour this over the oatmeal and sesame mixture and stir briskly. Add the walnuts, rosewater, turmeric and cardamom and mix well. Taste, and add sufficient syrup to sweeten to your liking, if using. Roll the mixture into 8 balls and serve warm.

Syrian Date Crescent Pastries

This recipe is a Syrian Jewish New Year speciality adapted to be made with wholefoods. The semolina gives the pastry an interesting knobbly texture and the marmalade lends a vital hint of orange to the very sweet date and walnut filling — designed, no doubt, to wish guests a sweet New Year.

MAKES ABOUT 24

For the pastry
225 g/8 oz/2 scant cups fine wholemeal flour, sifted
110 g/4 oz/1 scant cup wholemeal semolina flour
pinch of sea salt
225 g/8 oz/1 cup unsalted butter *or* non-hydrogenated margarine
1½ tbsp fresh lemon juice
1 tbsp oil
up to 120 ml/4 fl oz/½ cup cold water

For the filling
350 g/12 oz/3 cups stoned dates
75 g/3 oz/⅔ cup well-chopped walnuts
2 tbsp no-added-sugar marmalade, or more, to taste
pinch of ground cinnamon

For the glaze
2 tbsp brown rice syrup
2 tbsp water

Combine the flour, semolina flour and salt. Rub the butter or margarine into the flour until the mixture resembles large breadcrumbs (you can do this quickly in a food processor). Add the lemon juice, oil and then the water, a little at a time, until the dough is smooth and pliable. Leave it to stand for 10 minutes while the semolina absorbs the water, then chill, wrapped in unplasticized cling film, while you make the filling.

To make the filling, put the dates into a small saucepan and add water to barely cover. Boil the dates, uncovered, skimming off any foam that may form, until they are soft (about 10 minutes). Mash the dates to a paste, checking for any rogue stones, then lower the heat and stir until the water has been absorbed and the paste thickens. Add the walnuts, marmalade and cinnamon. Dates can vary in sweetness, so taste to be sure you can detect a hint of marmalade and, if not, add more by tablespoonfuls until it can definitely be tasted. Leave the filling to cool before using.

Pre-heat the oven to 190°C/375°F/Gas Mark 5. With your hands roll the chilled pastry dough into balls about 2.5 cm/1 in in diameter, then roll these out to form circles 9 cm/3½ in in diameter. Put a heaped teaspoon of filling into the centre of each then fold the dough over it. Crimp the edges together to make a tight seal, then bend them into crescent shapes. Place them on 2 ungreased baking trays, mix the glaze ingredients together and brush the crescents with it. Bake in the pre-heated oven for 25 minutes, then cool them on a wire rack. Store in an airtight container and eat within a week.

Kadeiffi

This beguiling Turkish pastry, made throughout the Middle East, is named after the crunchy strands of dough that are formed into a cylinder and filled with nuts. Until brown rice syrup was available, it was impossible to make a vegan, no-added-sugar version of any of the Greek, Turkish or Arab sweets. The syrup tastes very much like honey and provides nearly the same degree of sweetness as sugar. This is a quick version using Shredded Wheat, so the pastry is wholemeal and ready made.

Makes 6

For the cylinders
3 original size Shredded Wheat
50 g/2 oz/¼ cup butter or non-hydrogenated margarine (not SuperSpread), plus extra for greasing

For the filling
measuring by filling to the 250 ml/8 fl oz/1 cup mark of a measuring jug choose any combination of chopped, unsalted pistachios, toasted sesame seeds, desiccated coconut, chopped walnuts, almonds or hazelnuts
2 tsp cinnamon
½ tbsp organic brown rice syrup

For the syrup
110 g/4 oz/⅓ cup organic brown rice syrup
85 ml/3 fl oz/⅓ cup water
1 tsp lemon juice
few drops of rosewater (optional)

Pre-heat the oven to 180°C/350°F/Gas Mark 4 and grease a small baking tin with butter or margarine.

Holding the Shredded Wheat over the tin, hollow out most of their centres with a sharp knife (leaving the straggly centres in the tin with them).

Prepare your choice of filling and mix with the cinnamon and brown rice syrup.

Melt the butter or margarine gently in a pan, then add 2 tablespoons of it to the filling and mix in well. With a pastry brush, paint the Shredded Wheat with the remaining butter or margarine, both outside and inside. Now stuff the filling right inside the hollowed out Shredded Wheat and dot any left over around them, then bake the Kadeiffi in the pre-heated oven for 10 minutes until lightly browned. Leave them to cool for 5 minutes in the pan.

Meanwhile, make the syrup by combining the brown rice syrup, water and lemon juice in a saucepan. Bring to the boil, then reduce the heat and simmer, uncovered for 10–15 minutes until it has thickened slightly. Stir occasionally and let it cool a little. Spoon the warm syrup over the Kadeiffi, carefully covering the tops of each and leave to cool.

When the Kadeiffi are completely cool, slice each one in half and decorate with the bits of filling and loose strands surrounding them. These are best eaten the same or the next day and stored at room temperature, covered.

Chestnut Sultana and Peanut Pastries

Combining chestnuts, sultanas and peanuts in pastry is an Italian idea. Here, the filling is rolled and then cut, making a shape called 'bear claws', a wholly inappropriate name for this dainty and elegant treat.

MAKES ABOUT 20

For the pastry
175 g/6 oz/1¼ cups fine wholemeal flour
75 g/3 oz/⅓ cup butter or non-hydrogenated margarine, plus extra for greasing

tiny pinch of sea salt
2 tbsp lemon juice
2 tbsp brown rice syrup
2–3 tbsp cold water

For the filling
175 g/6 oz/1¼ cups sultanas
200 g/7 oz/⅝ cup crunchy peanut butter
235 g/8½ oz/1 scant cup unsalted, unsweetened chestnut purée
2½ tsp ground cinnamon
2½ tbsp brown rice syrup
1¼ tsp soya *or* cows' milk

For the glaze
1 tbsp brown rice syrup
1 tbsp water

First, make the pastry. Mix the flour and butter or margarine in a food processor or by hand, by rubbing the fat into the flour until the mixture resembles breadcrumbs. Add the salt, lemon juice, brown rice syrup and enough water to mix. If the dough seems dry, add a further tablespoon of water. Rest the dough in a plastic bag or covered bowl in the fridge for 15 minutes.

Meanwhile, pre-heat the oven to 200°C/400°F/Gas Mark 6 and grease a baking tray.

Also, make the filling. Chop the sultanas by hand or in a food processor, then blend them into the remaining ingredients.

Cut the pastry in half and return half to the fridge. Roll the other half out as thinly as possible to form a large rectangle, placing cling film or a plastic bag underneath and on top. Cut it into 10-cm/4-in wide strips across the rectangle, from short side to side. Roll the filling into a long sausage shape about 3 cm/1¼ in thick. Place a length of it down the centre of each strip and roll the edges of the pastry up and over it, to encase it, then seal the edges. Turn each of these over so that the seam is underneath. Cut each roll into 7.5-cm/3-in thick slices, then cut each of these halfway to the centre twice and fan the 'claws' out slightly. Place these on the greased baking tray. Mix the glaze ingredients together and brush each pastry with it, then bake them in the pre-heated oven for 25 minutes or until golden brown. Transfer them to a wire rack to cool. Store in an airtight container and eat within a week.

Jam Tarts

Try any pure fruit spread you like in these, and any pastry recipe will also do. The following recipe works very well as it results in a stiff case that holds the pure fruit spread, perfectly.

Makes 2 small tarts

For the pastry
225 g/8 oz/scant 2 cups wholemeal flour
pinch of sea salt
50 g/2 oz/⅓ scant cup SuperSpread *or* 5 tbsp vegetable oil, plus extra for greasing
2 tsp fresh lemon juice
3–5 tbsp cold water

For the filling
1 × 283-g/10-oz jar apricot *or* raspberry *or* strawberry pure fruit spread

Pre-heat the oven to 200°C/400°F/Gas Mark 6, and grease two 18–20-cm/7–8-in pie tins.

Put the flour and salt in a large bowl and mix. Add the SuperSpread or oil and lemon juice and rub in or mix well. Add 5 tablespoons of cold water if using SuperSpread or 3 tablespoons if using oil, adding it gradually until you have a manageable dough.

Divide the dough in half. Roll each half out to form an 18–20-cm/7–8-in round, making quarter turns after each roll. Place them in the prepared pie-tins and trim the edges.

Break up the pure fruit spread in the jar, spread half of it in each pastry case, then bake in the pre-heated oven for 25–30 minutes or until the pastry has lightly browned. Leave them to cool before eating and store in the fridge if not eaten that day.

Linzertorte

This rich, Austrian, raspberry tart has a ground almond or hazelnut pastry case. Although almonds are traditional, hazelnuts are delicious in wholemeal pastry. The flavour of this tart improves if it is kept for a day before serving.

Serves 6–8

For the pastry
90 g/3½ oz/⅞ cup fine wholemeal flour
½ tsp baking powder
1 tsp ground cinnamon
pinch of ground cloves
1 tsp carob powder
pinch of sea salt
75 g/3 oz/⅞ ground almonds *or* hazelnuts
65 g/2½ oz/⅓ cup butter *or* non-hydrogenated margarine, plus extra for greasing
½ tsp finely grated lemon zest
1½ tsp lemon juice *and* up to 1 tsp water
few drops of almond essence (optional)
4 tbsp brown rice syrup

For the filling
2 tbsp ground nuts, plus 1 tbsp, to decorate (optional)
215 g/7½ oz/¾ cup raspberry pure fruit spread

Make the pastry first. If using a food processor, simply mix all the pastry ingredients together. If making by hand, sift the flour, baking powder, spices, carob and salt into a bowl and add the ground nuts, then rub in the butter or margarine until the mixture resembles fine breadcrumbs. Stir in the lemon zest, lemon juice, water, almond essence and brown rice syrup and mix to a smooth dough. Roll the dough into a ball, wrap in a plastic bag or cling film and chill for an hour.

Pre-heat the oven to 180°C/350°F/Gas Mark 4 and grease a 23-cm/9-in pie tin.

Roll out three-quarters of the dough on a lightly floured surface to a thickness of 3 mm/⅛ in and press into the prepared pie tin. fluting the edges (if you have used margarine, the dough will be softer, so it will be necessary to roll it out between pieces of cling film or plastic bags).

Next, fill the pastry case. Evenly distribute two-thirds of the ground nuts over the base of the pastry case, then spread the raspberry spread over the top. Roll out the remaining dough into a rectangle and cut it into lattice strips (with a crinkly cutter if you have one). Lay the strips, first, in parallel lines then a second layer across these to make a lattice. Bake the Linzertorte in the pre-heated oven for 35–40 minutes and leave to cool completely before cutting. Scatter the remaining ground nuts over the top to decorate, if using.

Bakewell Tart

The original Bakewell tart is said to have come from Bakewell in Derbyshire and was made with apricot or peach preserves, candied orange peel and a custard flavoured with lemon rind and brandy, plus of course a lot of sugar and eggs.
Here is a much healthier, wholefood, no-added-sugar recipe, with a choice of jam combinations. Favourites are cherry or raspberry and Lemon Shred or the all-Lemon Shred version, but all are delicious.

Makes 1

For the pastry
75 g/3 oz/⅝ cup fine wholemeal flour
tiny pinch of salt
40 g/1½ oz/⅜ cup butter or non-hydrogenated margarine, plus extra for greasing
1 tbsp lemon juice
1 tbsp brown rice syrup
1–2 tbsp cold water

Bottom layer
4 tsp ground almonds
4 tbsp cherry or raspberry or strawberry or apricot pure fruit spread or Lemon Shred or Orange shred

Top layer
40 g/1½ oz/3 tbsp butter or non-hydrogenated margarine
5 tbsp Lemon Shred (or, if using Orange Shred on the bottom layer, use apricot pure fruit spread in this layer)
1 tsp arrowroot or use 1 beaten egg in place of the soya milk, baking powder and arrowroot
4 tbsp soya milk
½ tsp baking powder
65 g/2½ oz/¾ cup ground almonds
4 tbsp flaked almonds

First, make the pastry. If using a food processor, mix all the ingredients for the pastry, except the water. If making by hand, sift the flour and salt into a bowl and rub the butter or margarine into the flour until the mixture resembles breadcrumbs. Add the lemon juice, and brown rice syrup. For either method, next add 1 tablespoon of cold water to mix. If the dough seems dry add a further 1 tablespoon of water. Rest the dough for 15 minutes in the fridge.

Pre-heat the oven to 180°C/350°F/Gas Mark 4 and grease a 15--18-cm/6–7-in pie tin. Roll the dough out, between sheets of cling film or plastic bags, making it thin enough to fit the prepared pie tin. Trim the edges, then scatter the ground almonds over the base.

Spread your choice of pure fruit spread or Orange or Lemon Shred for the bottom layer of the filling on top of the ground almonds.

In a saucepan, prepare the top layer of the filling. Heat the butter or margarine and Lemon Shred or apricot spread. Dissolve the arrowroot in the soya milk, add the baking powder and add this mixture to the pan. Heat until the mixture has thickened, stirring constantly, then stir in the ground almonds (if you are using an egg instead, just heat the butter or margarine and pure fruit spread, remove the pan from the heat, then stir in the ground almonds and the beaten egg). Spoon this over the bottom layer, smoothing the top, then scatter the flaked almonds over. Bake in the pre-heated oven for 35–40 minutes until the top is delicately golden brown. Leave it to cool before serving.

Marmalade Marzipan Cake

This very adult-tasting cake is assembled rather than baked, and ready to eat in no time. Attracted by this quality, a friend asked for variations that her four-year-old daughter would enjoy eating, so that they could make it together. It is worth trying your favourite pure fruit spread in the Pineapple Marzipan Cake variation recipe, plus a complementary flavouring.

Serves 6–8

275 g/10 oz/2½ cups ground almonds, plus extra, if necessary
5 tbsp apple juice concentrate
up to 1½ tbsp water
2 tsp coriander seeds
1 × 283-g/10-oz jar Orange Shred (sweet 'n' fruity)
150 g/5 oz/⅔ cup low-fat cows' milk yogurt *or* soya yogurt with 2 tsp lemon juice stirred in (because it is milder)
75 g/3 oz/1 cup desiccated coconut, plus extra, if necessary
2 tbsp pumpkin seeds (optional)

Put half the ground almonds into a bowl or a food processor, add half of the apple juice concentrate and mix slowly, adding as much of the water as necessary to achieve the consistency of marzipan. Set aside 1 heaped tablespoon of the mixture for decoration. Press the remainder into the base of a small pie dish. Crush the coriander seeds until split in half (with a pestle and mortar or the back of a spoon), sprinkle them evenly over the top of the marzipan and press them in.

Mix half the marmalade into the yogurt, then add the coconut and remaining ground almonds. If you are using soya yogurt, add more ground almonds and coconut until the mixture is stiff. Spread this mixture over the marzipan layer.

Make little oranges (about 5 mm/¼ in in diameter) from the reserved marzipan and scatter these over the top of the cake. Melt the remaining marmalade with all but ½ tablespoon of the remaining apple juice concentrate over a low heat for a few seconds. Immediately, spoon this over the little oranges once, then a second time, then cover the rest of the cake. Leave it to cool.

Arrange the pumpkin seeds, if using, in the shape of an orange tree around the marzipan oranges or just put a single pumpkin seed in each little orange itself. Chill until you are ready to serve.

Variations

Pineapple Marzipan Cake For this, use pineapple pure fruit spread, but 425 g/15 oz/1½ jars are needed. Use a full jar's contents in the yogurt mixture and only 3 tablespoons of yogurt. Replace the coriander seeds with 2 tbsp cherry pure fruit spread. For the melted topping use 1 tablespoon of apple juice concentrate instead of 2 with the remaining spread. Consider using the pumpkin seeds to make leaves for a large marzipan pineapple.

Lemon and Kiwi Marzipan Cake For this variation, use 425 g/15 oz/1½ jars Kiwi pure fruit spread all together. Use a full jar's contents in the yogurt mixture made with just 3 tablespoons of yogurt. Use the grated zest of 1 small lemon instead of the coriander seeds in the centre, saving half of it to sprinkle on top of the melted spread. Consider decorating the cake with slices of kiwi fruit and glazing these with the remaining spread and 1 tablespoon of apple juice concentrate.

BISCUITS, SWEETS, CAKES AND OTHER TREATS

Rice Puff Crunch

A treat that is ready in 15 minutes, Rice Puff Crunch appeals to adults as well as children.

Makes 4–8

1 tbsp vegetable oil *or* SuperSpread, plus extra for greasing
2 tbsp maize malt syrup *or* brown rice syrup *or* barley malt
½ tsp ground cinnamon
1–2 tbsp chopped roasted hazelnuts *or* peanuts (optional)
40 g/1½ oz/1 cup Organic Rice Puffs

Pre-heat the oven to 180°C/350°F/Gas Mark 4 and grease a 20-cm/8-in pie plate or cake tin.

Heat the oil or SuperSpread with the syrup in a medium-sized saucepan until bubbly, stirring constantly (about 30 seconds). Remove the pan from the heat.

Quickly add the cinnamon, nuts and Organic Rice Puffs and stir until everything is well coated. Spread the mixture out in the prepared pie plate, or cake tin, making as thin a layer as possible. Bake it in the pre-heated oven for 10 minutes, or 15 minutes if you are using SuperSpread. Leave it to cool a little, then using a palette knife, lift it out, whole, on to a plate. When it has cooled completely, break it into smaller pieces (if the Crunch should get stuck in the tin, warm it slightly over the hob and lift it out).

Variation: Peanut Butter Puff Crunch

Add 1 tablespoon of crunchy or smooth peanut butter when heating the oil or SuperSpread and syrup, and leave out the cinnamon and nuts. Bake it for 10 minutes. This is more brittle and harder to break than the one above.

Cinnamon, Walnut and Marmalade Layer Cake

Even though there are no eggs used in the making of it, this layer cake has an excellent texture. The marmalade glaze on top shines and the sultanas and walnuts dotted through and on top tie it all together. It can be made very quickly in a food processor.
Note that you can substitute 175 g/6 oz/½ cup brown rice syrup for the barley malt and apple juice concentrate if you like a sweeter cake, but you will need to bake it a little longer.

SERVES 6

For the cake
oil, for greasing
110 g/4 oz/½ cup light tahini (any separated oil poured off)
250 ml/8 fl oz/1 cup orange juice
75 g/3 oz/¼ cup organic barley malt
50 g/2 oz/¼ cup apple juice concentrate
200 g/7 oz/1½ cups wholemeal flour, plus extra for flouring
1 tsp baking powder
½ tsp bicarbonate of soda
¼ tsp sea salt
1 tsp ground cinnamon, plus extra for dusting
65 g/2½ oz/½ cup sultanas *or* raisins, plus 1 tbsp, to decorate
40 g/1½ oz/½ cup walnuts, chopped, plus 2 tbsp, to decorate

For the glaze
6 tbsp no-added-sugar marmalade
3 tbsp organic barley malt *or* maize syrup *or* brown rice syrup
3 tbsp non-hydrogenated margarine *or* butter

Pre-heat the oven to 180°C/350°F/Gas Mark 4 and grease and flour two 20-cm/8-in cake tins.

Put the tahini into a food processor or bowl. Add the orange juice and mix them together. Add the barley malt and apple juice concentrate and mix. Add the dry ingredients, except the fruit and nuts, and mix. Stir in the sultanas or raisins and chopped walnuts, reserving those to be used for decoration.

Divide the mixture evenly between the two prepared tins and

smooth it out to the edges. Bake in the pre-heated oven for 25–30 minutes. Leave them to cool in the tins, then remove them to a plate.

Melt the ingredients for the glaze together in a saucepan and pour half of it over one cake. Scatter half the remaining walnuts over and dust with cinnamon. Put the second cake on top, repeat, this time sprinkling the remaining sultanas or raisins over as well.

Carob Layer Cake with Peanut Butter Icing

This is a light sponge flavoured with carob and coffee, filled and topped with a rich peanut and date icing. Make the icing as soon as the cake is in the oven, so it will cool in time to use. The cake can be made in a food processor for speed.

SERVES 6

For the cake
oil, for greasing
165 g/5½ oz/1 cup dates, stoned
120 ml/4 fl oz/½ cup water
1 tsp decaffeinated instant coffee
50 g/2 oz/¼ cup smooth peanut butter
4 tbsp non-hydrogenated margarine *or* SuperSpread *or* butter
2 tsp vanilla essence
1 tbsp cider *or* wine vinegar
300 ml/10 fl oz/1 cup + 3 tbsp soya milk
200 g/7 oz/1¾ cups wholemeal flour
¾ tsp sea salt
¾ tsp bicarbonate of soda
50 g/2 oz/½ cup carob

For the filling and the icing
150 g/5 oz/1 cup dates, stoned
250 ml/8 fl oz/1 cup soya milk
225 g/8 oz/1 cup smooth peanut butter
5 tbsp non-hydrogenated margarine *or* butter
2 tbsp desiccated coconut (optional)

Pre-heat the oven to 180°C/350°F/Gas Mark 4, and grease two 20–23-cm/8–9-in cake tins.

Boil the dates in the water. Remove 1 tablespoon of the hot water to a cup and dissolve the instant coffee in it. Continue to boil the dates until they are soft and the water has evaporated.

Check for any remaining stones, then whizz in a liquidizer or food processor or press through a sieve, then stir in the coffee.

Add the peanut butter, margarine or SuperSpread or butter and vanilla and mix in.

Stir the vinegar into the soya milk to curdle it.

Sift the flour, together with the salt, bicarbonate of soda and carob into a bowl, or just add them to the food processor. Add the dry mixture to the date mixture alternately with the soured soya milk a third at a time.

Pour the cake batter into the prepared cake tins, dividing it equally between them and smoothing the tops. Bake in the pre-heated oven for 25 minutes, or until a knife inserted into the centre comes out clean. Leave the cakes to cool on a wire rack before icing.

While the cakes are cooking, make the filling and icing.

Heat the dates with the soya milk until they are soft, stirring regularly. Mash the dates well, removing any remaining stones.

Add the peanut butter and margarine or butter to the pan and stir until the mixture has melted and is thick and smooth. Leave it to cool before using.

Spread half the icing over one of the cakes, sandwich the second on top, then ice it. Sprinkle the coconut on top, if using.

Plum and Walnut Bread

This recipe has survived from an early Whole Earth leaflet. It is a sweet, moist, fruity bread, or pudding, and makes use of an interesting method of assembly.

MAKES ONE 450-G/1-LB TEABREAD

oil, for greasing
75 g/3 oz/⅓ cup non-hydrogenated margarine *or* SuperSpread
1 × 283-g/10-oz jar Golden Plum pure fruit spread
50 g/2 oz/½ cup sultanas
50 g/2 oz/½ cup prunes, stones removed, chopped, *or* raisins
110 g/4 oz/¾ cup dates, stones removed, chopped
110 g/4 oz/¾ cup wholemeal flour
1 tsp baking powder
¼ tsp bicarbonate of soda
¼–½ tsp mixed spice
50 g/2 oz/½ cup walnuts, chopped, plus some whole pieces, to decorate

Pre-heat the oven to 160°C/325°F/Gas Mark 3 and grease a 450-g/1-lb loaf tin.

Melt the margarine in a saucepan and mix in all but 2 tablespoons of the Golden Plum spread. Add all the dried fruit and cook gently until it is soft. If you are using SuperSpread, cook the fruit in the pure fruit spread, *then* stir in the SuperSpread until well blended.

Meanwhile, combine the flour, baking powder, bicarbonate of soda, mixed spice and walnuts (reserving those you will use to decorate the teabread) in a bowl or food processor. Add the fruity mixture and mix it in well. Pour it into the prepared loaf tin and smooth the surface with the back of a spoon. Bake it in the pre-heated oven for 35–40 minutes or until a knife inserted into the centre comes out clean. Either serve it warm as a pudding with soya yogurt, or remove it from the tin, leave it to cool, then decorate it with the reserved walnuts. Heat the remaining Golden Plum spread and spoon it over the top to glaze.

Peanut Butter Sultana Bread

This is a light, quick bread, studded with sultanas, that is not at all sweet. The gluten-free version has a very light colour and delicious taste. Using cream of tartar, bicarbonate of soda and salt instead of baking powder works just as well and eliminates the aluminium used in most commercial brands of baking powder.

Makes one 450-g/1-lb loaf

oil, for greasing
110 g/4 oz/½ cup peanut butter
300 ml/10 fl oz/1¼ cups soya milk
175 g/6 oz/½ cup organic barley malt *or* maize syrup
235 g/8½ oz/2 cups wholemeal flour
1 tbsp cream of tartar
1½ tsp bicarbonate of soda
½ tsp sea salt
75 g/3 oz/¾ cup sultanas *or* raisins

Pre-heat the oven to 180°C/350°F/Gas Mark 4 and grease a 450-g/1-lb or 900-g/2-lb loaf tin.

Mix, in a food processor or by hand, the peanut butter, milk and barley malt or corn syrup. Add the flour, cream of tartar, bicarbonate of soda and salt and whizz or mix well. Stir in the sultanas or raisins, ensuring that they are well distributed.

Pour the mixture into the prepared loaf tin and bake in the pre-heated oven for 45–55 minutes, or until a knife inserted into the centre comes out clean. Remove the loaf from the tin and leave to cool on a wire rack.

Variation
For a gluten-free loaf, instead of the wholemeal flour use the following:

120 g/4½ oz/1 cup brown rice flour
100 g/4 oz/¾ cup cornmeal
15 g/½ oz/¼ cup soya flour

Peanut Butter Banana Bread

This is richer and more dense than the Peanut Sultana Bread (see page 142). It is actually more of a cake and is a real treat.

Makes one 450-g/1-lb loaf

oil, for greasing
75 g/3 oz/⅓ cup dates, stoned
3 tbsp water
50 g/2 oz/⅓ cup non-hydrogenated margarine *or* 75 g/3 oz SuperSpread
2 large *or* 3 small bananas, mashed
1 tsp vanilla essence
1 tbsp soya *or* cows' milk (but leave it out if using SuperSpread)
175 g/6 oz/1¼ cups wholemeal flour, sifted
¾ tsp bicarbonate of soda
1½ tsp cream of tartar
¼ tsp sea salt

Pre-heat the oven to 180°C/350°F/Gas Mark 4 and grease a 450-g/1-lb or 900-g/2-lb loaf tin.

Put the dates into a small saucepan with the water, heat and simmer until they have absorbed all the water. Check for any remaining stones. Mash them well by hand or in a food processor.

Add all the remaining ingredients to the food processor or bowl in the order in which they are listed and whizz or mix until combined.

Pour the mixture into the prepared loaf tin and bake in the pre-heated oven for 45–55 minutes, or until a knife inserted into the centre comes out clean. Remove the loaf from the tin and leave to cool on a wire rack.

Peanut Butter Muffins

Muffins take no time to mix and can be ready to eat in half an hour. These muffins have a mild peanut flavour and are only mildly sweet.

MAKES 16 SMALL OR 12 LARGE MUFFINS

oil, for greasing
225 g/8 oz/2 cups wholemeal flour
2 tsp baking powder
2 tsp soya flour
pinch of sea salt
2 tbsp SuperSpread *or* non-hydrogenated margarine
110 g/4 oz/½ cup peanut butter (preferably crunchy)
75 g/3 oz/⅓ cup organic brown rice syrup
250 ml/8 fl oz/1 cup soya *or* cows' milk

Pre-heat the oven to 190°C/375°F/Gas Mark 5 and line a muffin tin with fairy cakes cases or oil each cup individually.

Mix all the dry ingredients in a food processor or mix by hand, sifting the flour, baking powder, soya flour and salt together into a large bowl.

Beat the SuperSpread or margarine with the peanut butter, then add the brown rice syrup. Mix this into the flours, then add the milk.

Immediately, spoon the batter into the prepared muffin tin or fairy cake cases until it just reaches the edge. Bake in the pre-heated oven for 25 minutes, or until a knife inserted into the centre comes out cleanly. Remove them from the muffin tin and leave to cool on a wire rack. Serve warm with butter, non-hydrogenated margarine or SuperSpread. Otherwise, store in an airtight container and eat within 2 days.

Strawberry Shortcake

American shortcake is a soft, no-egg cake, sandwiched with conserves or fresh fruit and traditionally topped with whipped cream. This wholefood version is delicious just with strawberry pure fruit spread. However, a little real whipped cream on top would not go amiss. Alternatively, try the vegan SuperSpread Cream, which tastes like vanilla custard mixed with thick cream. This recipe can be made and baked within 25 minutes.

Serves 4–6

225 g/8 oz/2 cups wholemeal flour
2 tsp bicarbonate of soda
1 tsp cream of tartar
¼ tsp sea salt
6 tbsp SuperSpread *or* 4 tbsp butter *or* non-hydrogenated margarine
and 2 tbsp oil
4 tbsp apple juice concentrate *or* maize *or* organic brown rice syrup
120 ml/4 fl oz/½ cup soya *or* cows' milk
1 tbsp SuperSpread *or* melted butter *or* non-hydrogenated margarine,
plus extra for greasing
1 × 283-g/10-oz jar strawberry pure fruit spread, to serve
450 ml/15 fl oz whipping cream, whipped, *or* SuperSpread Cream
(see below), to serve

For the SuperSpread Cream
95 g/3¾ oz/½ cup SuperSpread
3 tbsp soya milk
2 tbsp brown rice syrup
1 tsp vanilla essence

Pre-heat the oven to 220°C/425°F/Gas Mark 7 and grease a 23-cm/9-in pie dish.

If you are using SuperSpread, simply mix all the ingredients together by hand or in a food processor. If you are using butter or margarine, combine the dry ingredients first, then cut in either the butter or margarine and add apple juice concentrate or syrup and milk to form a dough.

Press half the dough into the prepared pie dish with greased fingers or a knife. Spread the 1 tablespoon of SuperSpread or melted butter or non-hydrogenated margarine over the top, then cover with the remaining dough and smooth the top. Score it into six pieces with a fork and bake in the pre-heated oven for 15–20 minutes, then check that a knife inserted into the centre comes out clean. Cool it in the pan, then cover it well to prevent it drying out.

To serve, cut the shortcake along the scored lines, then slice each piece in half where the two halves of the dough were sandwiched together and fill with the strawberry pure fruit spread. Using an electric whisk, whip all the SuperSpread Cream ingredients together until light and foamy. Put on top of biscuit, together with a dollop of strawberry pure fruit spread. Or, use real cream, whipped, if preferred.

DRINKS

Apricot Ice-Cream Soda

A fruity, low-calorie treat for a warm afternoon in the garden. If you are in a hurry whizz all the ingredients together with two ice cubes for apricot milkshakes.

Serves 4

475 ml/16 fl oz/2 cups soya milk
750 ml/1¼ pints/3 cups no-added-sugar Real Lemonade
1 × 283-g/10-oz jar apricot pure fruit spread
apple juice concentrate, to taste
12–16 fresh mint leaves (optional)
4 sprigs of mint, to decorate (optional)

In a liquidizer or food processor whizz together all the ingredients, except the sprigs of mint. Pour half the mixture into a shallow tray and freeze for at least 1 hour, or until solid. Put the other half of the mixture in the fridge.

Whizz or beat the frozen mixture to break up the crystals, then divide it between 4 glasses. Pour the chilled mixture over the ice-cream and decorate with the sprigs of mint, if using.

Per person
120 ml/4 fl oz/½ cup soya milk
175 ml/6 fl oz/¾ cup Real Lemonade
4 tbsp apricot pure fruit spread
3–4 fresh mint leaves (optional)
sprig of mint, to decorate (optional)

Peanut Butter and Jam Thick Milkshakes

When made with soya milk, these milkshakes are as thick as the fast-food ones where the straw stands up by itself. If you prefer them thinner, use half the amount of jam and sweeten to taste with further apple juice concentrate. Unlike the fast-food shakes, though, these are full of protein and have no artificial additives, colours, flavourings or sweeteners.

Makes 4

1 × 312-g/11-oz jar *or* 1⅛ cups smooth peanut butter
1 × 283-g/10-oz jar *or* 1 cup Hedgerow *or* blueberry pure fruit spread
3 tbsp apple juice concentrate
1 1/1¾ pints/4 cups soya *or* cows' milk

Put the peanut butter, Hedgerow or blueberry spread and apple juice concentrate together in a food processor and whizz. Slowly add the milk (if you are using a liquidizer, whizz all the ingredients together in two lots). Either chill, or use chilled ingredients for instant milkshakes.

Per person
4 tbsp smooth peanut butter
4 tbsp Hedgerow or blueberry pure fruit spread
¾ tbsp apple juice concentrate
250 ml/8 fl oz/1 cup soya *or* cows' milk

Berry Smoothie

A smoothie is an all-fruit drink with the consistency of a milkshake. Any of the berry pure fruit spreads will be delicious in this.

Serves 4
425 g/15 oz/1½ cups Hedgerow pure fruit spread
2 ripe bananas, cut into chunks
120 ml/4 fl oz/½ cup apple juice
crushed ice (optional)

In a food processor or liquidizer, whizz the Hedgerow spread and bananas until smooth. Then add the apple juice and whizz again.

Pour over crushed ice, if using, in four 250-ml/8 fl-oz capacity glasses and serve immediately.

Per person
6 tbsp Hedgerow pure fruit spread
½ ripe banana, cut into chunks
2 tbsp apple juice

Fruity Frothy Milkshakes

Here's something special for a snack. These milkshakes are best made with soya milk because, for some reason, there is no aftertaste when soya milk mixes with fruit, but there is quite a marked one if cows' milk is used.

Per person
250 ml/8 fl oz/1 cup soya milk
150 g/5 oz/½ cup/½ jar any pure fruit spread (except apricot — see page 146 for recipe for Apricot Ice-Cream Soda) *or* Lemon *or* Orange Shred
apple juice concentrate, to taste, if necessary

Just mix the soya milk and fruit spread in a liquidizer or food processor until frothy. A touch of apple juice concentrate to taste may be needed for some jams.

Fruity Party Punch

Fizzy, fruity and just sweet enough, this is a totally natural, junk-free drink for children's or adults' parties.

Serves 6–8

2 × 250-ml/8 fl-oz bottles no-added-sugar Orange Soda
1 × 250-ml/8 fl-oz bottle no-added-sugar Real Lemonade
1 × 283-g/10-oz jar strawberry pure fruit spread
250 ml/8 fl oz/1 cup water
apple juice concentrate, to taste

Chill all the ingredients in advance, if possible.

Whisk the sodas into the pure fruit spread in a large bowl and add the water or whizz all the ingredients in a food processor. Add a little apple juice concentrate if necessary. Chill the punch until using. For adults, use the full-strength recipe and serve over ice (or spike with gin or vodka). For children, dilute it with a further 120 ml/4 fl oz/½ cup water and, if they are finicky, sieve the strawberry pure fruit spread to remove the pips before mixing it in.

Spicy Vegetable Cocktail

This makes a savoury start to a meal or an excellent liquid lunch for two.

Serves 2–4

½ cucumber
2 celery sticks
1–2 tbsp chopped onion *or* 1 spring onion
1 small clove garlic
2 heaped tbsp organic no-added-sugar ketchup
½ tsp ground cumin
900 ml/½ pint/1¼ cups iced water *or* vegetable stock
ice cubes and celery leaves, to decorate (optional)

Chop the cucumber and celery into large pieces. Put all the ingredients, except the ice cubes and celery leaves, into a blender and whizz until smooth (a food processor will do this job, but add the water or stock *after* whizzing the vegetables).

Pour it into glasses, add an ice cube to each and decorate with celery leaves.

Warm, Frothy Orange

This delicate, orange-scented hot drink is practically instant and very warming. The soya milk becomes frothy and makes a delicious combination with the Orange Soda.

SERVES 4

2 × 250-ml/8-fl oz bottles/2¼ cups no-added-sugar Orange Soda
250 ml/8 fl oz/1⅛ cups soya milk
8 cloves (optional, for added warmth and spice)

Pour 1 bottle of Orange Soda and all of the soya milk into a saucepan (with the cloves, if using) and heat gently until bubbly (2–3 minutes; if left too long, it will boil over, so keep an eye on it). Remove it from the heat, add the second bottle of Orange Soda, then pour it into 4 mugs, distributing the froth equally.

Hot Pineapple and Ginger

This is a warming drink in the winter or for whenever you feel under the weather. It's easy to have fresh ginger always at hand if you cut it into small pieces and freeze them. Shavings can even be taken off, as here, and the rest returned to the freezer.

SERVES 1

3 level tbsp pineapple pure fruit spread
a few thin shavings of fresh ginger

Put the jam into a mug, add boiling water to fill cup and stir to mix the spread through. Top with the ginger shavings and drink.

Variation: Hot Blackcurrant

Mixing 2 tablespoons of blackcurrant pure fruit spread with water is also delicious. Do not stop there — try any flavour or blends of pure fruit spread you have to hand.

MENU IDEAS

Quick Dinner Party Recipes

STARTERS

Leeks in Marmalade Sauce
Spiced Marmalade Soup with Macadamia Nuts
Warm Apricot Soup with Walnuts
Hungarian Cherry Soup
Tart Peanut and Other Dips

MAIN COURSES

Hummus Pie with Sweet Peppers
Oil-Free Stir-Fried Vegetables with Toasted Hazelnuts
Apricot Risotto
Pistachio Risotto
Abargoo Rice

VEGETABLES

Cabbage with Marmalade and Juniper Berries
Hummus Cabbage Salad

DESSERTS

Hot Pineapple with Lemon Shred and Ginger
Rose Berries
Three Nut Truffles
Coconut Macaroons
Strawberry Shortcake

Planned Dinner Parties: Winter

STARTERS

Hot Peanut Butter Scones with Onion Salad
Gingered Peanut Soufflés
Onion-Smothered Smooth Pâté with Sesame Seeds
Chestnut and Pine Nut Pâté
Long-Simmered Mushrooms
Almond Soup
Roasted Nut Cream Soup with Green Peppercorns

MAIN COURSES

Roasted Peppers and Aubergines in a Hummus Crust
Pistachio Risotto
Buckwheat Noodles with Jerusalem Artichokes and Toasted Hazelnuts
Gram Flour Cumin Pancakes with Ginger Peanut Sauce and Coconut Chutney
Green Pea Cakes with Smoky Creole Sauce
Smoked Tofu with Barbecue Sauce
Lotus Leaf Steamed Rice Packages
Abargoo Rice

DESSERTS

Bread and Butter Pudding
Marmalade and Hot Fudge Crêpe Gâteaux
Linzertorte
Bakewell Tart
Kadeiffi
Sladké Knedlíky (Czech Sweet Dumplings)
Cinnamon Walnut and Marmalade Layer Cake

Planned Dinner Parties: Summer

STARTERS

Cold Sesame Noodles
Blackcurrant and Lemon Soup
Golden Soup
Avocado and Lemonade Soup with Tarragon Ice Flakes

Main Courses and Salads

Hummus Pie with Sweet Peppers
California Sushi Nori Rolls
Glass Noodle Salad
Hummus Pizza with Fresh Herbs
Salad of Radicchio and Rocket with Artichokes and Walnuts
Green and Yellow Salad with Apricot and Lime Dressing
Sweet-Sour Carrot Salad
Spinach Soufflés

Desserts

Banana Ice-Cream Pie with Hot Fudge Sauce
Cherry Ice-Cream
Peach Melba Granita
Two Ice-Creams That Go Like A Bombe
Marmalade Marzipan Cake
Strawberry and Almond Ice-cCream
Fruity Fools
Pineapple Sorbet with Cherries

Instant and Quick Recipes

Tomato and Bean Soup
Organic Cream of Tomato Soup
Warm Hummus Soup
Hungarian Cherry Soup
Kensington Soup
Ten-minute Vegetable Stew Italiano
Baked Bean Pancakes
Apricot Risotto
Walnut and Caper Rice Salad
Quick and Different Baked Beans
Oil-Free Stir-Fried Vegetables
Rice and Peas
Hummus Cabbage Salad
Quick Fruit Pudding
Fruity Fools
Quick Rice Pudding

Children's Specialities

Grilled Sandwiches
Ketchup and Mustard Burgers
Jam Tarts
Peanut Butter Fudge
Rice Puff Crunch
Peanut Butter Cookies
Ginger Snaps
Peanut Butter and Blueberry Ice-Cream
Carob Layer Cake with Peanut Icing
Fruity Frothy Milkshakes
Peanut Butter and Jam Thick Milkshakes
Fruity Party Punch

Buffet Parties

Tart Peanut Dip for Crudités
Creamy Peanut Onion Dip
Long-Simmered Mushrooms
Cold Sesame Noodles
Motley Bean Salad
Picnic Potato Salad
Curried Apple Salad
Blackcurrant Salad Mould with Chinese Leaf
Lemonade Jelly with Marigolds
Chestnut and Pine Nut Pâté
Creamy, Herby Rice Loaf
Georgian Kidney Beans with Plum Vinaigrette
Syrian Date Crescents
Chestnut and Peanut Butter Pastries
Peanut Banana Bread
Fruity Party Punch

Where to Find the Products Mentioned in this Book

Your local health food shop can order any of the items mentioned in this book. Distributors will make up orders and supply single bottles of most things to shops.

The Soil Association prints regional guides to health food shops and organic suppliers (£2.50 in 1994). They also have a database of farm shops. They can be contacted at the following address:

The Soil Association
86–88 Colston Street
Bristol
Avon BS1 5BB
Tel: 0272 290661

The following companies supply a wide range of health foods by mail order:

Countryside Wholefoods Limited
19 Forty Hill
Enfield
Middlesex EN2 9HT
Tel: 081-363 2933
(Greater London Area)
Tel: 0992 441961 (nationwide, for orders and price list)

They supply the complete range of Whole Earth products and deliver free in the Greater London area. They will also deliver organic vegetables. There is a small charge for delivery elsewhere in mainland UK, but liquids in glass bottles and vegetables cannot be delivered to these areas.

Freshlands Mail Order
196 Old Street
London EC1V 9FR
Tel and fax: 071-490 3170

Whole Earth grain syrups and a wide range of macrobiotic and Japanese specialities can be ordered from Freshlands and a price list is available.

Peppercorn's Mail Order
2 Heath Street
London NW3 6TE
Tel: 081-444 5660

Telephone them for information about stock and prices.

Real Foods
37 Broughton Street
Edinburgh EH1 3JU
Tel: 031-557 1911

Send a SAE for a price list

Wild Oats Mail Order
210 Westbourne Grove
London W11 2RH
Tel: 071–229 1063
(Contact Vanessa Vine)

They will send the full range of Whole Earth, macrobiotic and organic products by post (except liquids in bottles). A price list is available.

Wholefoods Express Limited
95 Southgate Road
London N1 3JS
Tel: 071-354 4923

They stock the full range of Whole Earth products and wholefoods. There is a local delivery service or they will send items by mail order throughout the UK. A price list is available on application.

Further Reading

Carson, Rachel, *The Silent Spring* (Penguin, 1982)
The Food Magazine, published by The Food Commission, 3rd Floor, Viking House, 5–11 Worship Street, London EC2A 2BH; *Tel*: 071-628 7774
Griggs, Barbara, *The Food Factor* (Viking Books, 1986)
Lawrence, Felicity, ed., *Additives: Your Complete Survival Guide* (Century Hutchinson, 1986)
The London Food Commission, *Food Adulteration and How to Beat It* (Unwin Paperbacks, 1988)
Murray, M.T. and J.E. Pizzorno, *Encyclopaedia of Natural Medicine*, (Macdonald Optima Books, 1990)
Living Earth Magazine, published by The Soil Association, 86–88 Colston Street, Bristol, Avon BS1 5BB; *Tel*: 0272 290661
Taylor, Joan, and Derek Taylor, eds, *Safe Food Handbook* (Ebury Press, 1990)
Walker, Carol, and Geoffrey Cannon, *The Food Scandal*, (Century, 1984)
Webb, Tony, and Tim Lang, *Food Irradiation: Myth and Reality* (Thorsons, 1990)

Index

Abargoo rice, 69
almonds: almond soup, 37
  Bakewell tart, 134-5
  marmalade marzipan cake, 135-6
apples: baked apples three ways, 114
  curried apple salad, 54
apricots: apricot ice-cream soda, 146
  apricot pilaf, 70
  warm apricot soup with walnuts, 36
avocados: avocado and lemonade soup, 44
  sweet lemon and avocado cream, 111

baked beans: baked bean pancakes, 71
  golden rice burgers, 73
  hot and sour baked beans, 78
  hot grilled sandwiches, 80
  quick chilli, 79
  smoky baked bean cornbread pie, 68-9
Bakewell tart, 134-5
bananas: banana ice-cream pie, 100-1
  peanut butter banana bread, 143
beans: hot tamale pie, 76-7
  Kensington soup, 40
  motley bean salad or stew, 55
berry smoothie, 148
biscuits, 121-4
blackcurrant: blackcurrant and lemon soup, 45
  blackcurrant salad mould, 52
  blackcurrant sorbet, 108
blueberries: peanut butter and blueberry ice-cream, 103
bread and butter pudding, 116-17
broccoli with Super hollandaise, 99
Brussels sprouts and chestnuts in peanut sauce, 95
buckwheat, potato and dill casserole, 84
burgers: golden rice, 73
  ketchup and mustard, 72-3

cabbage: cabbage 'noodles', 85
cabbage with marmalade and juniper berries, 84
  hummus cabbage salad, 56
cakes, 135-40
California sushi nori rolls, 32-3
carob, 20

carob layer cake, 139-40
  marmalade and hot fudge crêpe gâteau, 119-20
carrots: in apricot mustard sauce, 93
  sweet lemon carrots, 93
  sweet-sour carrot salad, 48
cauliflower please, 87
cherries: cherry ice-cream, 102
  Hungarian cherry soup, 36-7
chestnuts: chestnut and pine nut pâté, 23
  chestnut sultana and peanut pastries, 130-1
chilli, quick, 79
chutney, coconut, 58-60
cinnamon, walnut and marmalade layer cake, 138-9
coconut: coconut chutney, 58-60
  coconut macaroons, 123
corn: mashed potatoes with grilled corn, garlic and dill, 90
cornbread pie, smoky baked bean, 68-9
crêpe gâteau, marmalade and hot fudge, 119-20
cucumber and onion salad, 51
curried apple salad, 54
Czech sweet dumplings, 118-19

date crescent pastries, Syrian, 128-9
desserts, 100-20
dips, 34-5
drinks, 146-50
dumplings: sladké knedlíky, 118-19

fat, 11-13
fools, fruity, 110
French beans with peanut sesame sauce, 96
fruit: berry smoothie, 148
  fruity fools, 110
  fruity frothy milkshakes, 148
  fruity party punch, 149
  quick fruit pudding, 113
  rose berries, 110-11
fudge, peanut butter, 126

Georgian kidney beans, 50
ginger: ginger nuts, 121
  ginger peanut sauce, 58-60
glass noodle salad, 65-6

golden soup, 45
gram flour cumin pancakes, 58-60
granita, Peach Melba, 108-9
grapefruit: fresh grapefruit with blackcurrant sauce, 30
  grilled grapefruit halves with cherries, 29
  grilled grapefruit with marmalade, 29
green and yellow salad, 47

helvah, Turkish-style, 127
hummus: hummus cabbage salad, 56
  hummus pie with sweet pepper, 63
  hummus pizza with fresh herbs, 74-5
  roasted peppers and aubergines in a hummus crust, 60-1
  warm hummus soup, 40-1
Hungarian cherry soup, 36-7

ice-cream: apricot ice-cream soda, 146
  banana ice-cream pie, 100-1
  cherry, 102
  peanut butter and blueberry, 103
  strawberry and almond, 106
  two ice-creams that go like a bombe, 104-5
ingredients, 19-20

jam tarts, 132
jelly: blackcurrant salad mould, 52
  lemonade jelly with marigolds, 48-9

kadeiffi, 129-30
Kensington soup, 40
kidney beans: Georgian, 50
  ketchup and mustard burgers, 72-3
  rice and peas, 81
kombu and mushroom casserole, 98

labels, 17-18
leeks in marmalade sauce, 30
lemon and avocado cream, sweet, 111
Lemon Shred, hot pineapple with ginger and, 117
lemonade jelly with marigolds, 48-9
Linzertorte, 132-3
lotus leaf packages, 64-5

macaroons, coconut, 123
marmalade: marmalade and hot fudge crêpe gâteau, 119-20
  marmalade marzipan cake, 135-6
  spiced marmalade soup, 38
marzipan cake, marmalade, 135-6

Meglie-Lebanese festive pudding, 112
menus, 151-4
milkshakes: fruity frothy, 148
  peanut butter and jam thick, 147
muffins, peanut butter, 144
mushrooms: kombu and mushroom casserole, 98
  long-simmered mushrooms, 25
  marinated mushrooms, 56
  mushroom and peanut stew, 85

noodles: buckwheat noodles with Jerusalem artichokes, 62
  cold sesame noodles, 31
  glass noodle salad, 65-6
  spinach noodle bake, 86
nori rolls, California sushi, 32-3
nut cream soup, roasted, 38-9

oils, 13
onion salad, 26-7
Orange Soda: warm, frothy orange, 150
oranges: St Clement's biscuits, 124
organic food, 14-15

pancakes: baked bean pancakes, 71
  gram flour cumin pancakes, 58-60
papaya with parsnip rémoulade, 28
parsnips: papaya with parsnip rémoulade, 28
  parsnips in creamy dressing, 92
pastries: chestnut sultana and peanut pastries, 130-1
  kadeiffi, 129-30
  Syrian date crescent pastries, 128-9
pâtés: chestnut and pine nut, 23
  onion-smothered smooth pâté, 24-5
Peach Melba granita, 108-9
peanut butter, 12, 19
  cream of peanut soup, 43
  creamy peanut onion dip, 34-5
  ginger peanut sauce, 58-60
  ginger peanut soufflés, 33
  hot peanut butter scones, 26-7
  onion-smothered smooth pâté, 24-5
  peanut butter and blueberry ice-cream, 103
  peanut butter and jam thick milkshakes, 147
  peanut butter banana bread, 143
  peanut butter cookies, 122-3
  peanut butter fudge, 126
  peanut butter muffins, 144

INDEX

peanut butter sultana bread, 142
tart peanut dip for crudités, 34
peas: green pea cakes, 66-7
peppers: roasted peppers and aubergines in a hummus crust, 60-1
pilaf, apricot, 70
pineapple: hot pineapple and ginger, 150
  hot pineapple with Lemon Shred and ginger, 117
  pineapple sorbet with cherries, 107
pistachio risotto, 57
pizza, hummus with fresh herbs, 74-5
plum and walnut bread, 141
potatoes: mashed potatoes with grilled corn, garlic and dill, 90
  picnic potato salad, 53
  potato, buckwheat and dill casserole, 84
  reduced calorie parsley potato salad, 53
  smooth potato soup, 41
punch, fruity party, 149

radicchio, salad of rocket and, 46-7
raspberries: Linzertorte, 132-3
  raspberry and apricot frozen yogurt parfaits, 109
rice: Abargoo rice, 69
  apricot pilaf, 70
  California sushi nori rolls, 32-3
  golden rice burgers, 73
  herby, creamy rice loaf, 82-3
  pistachio risotto, 57
  quick rice pudding, 115
  rice and peas, 81
  walnut and caper rice salad, 49
rice flour: Meglie-Lebanese festive pudding, 112
Rice Puff crunch, 137
rose berries, 110-11
runner beans in mustard sauce, 97

St Clement's biscuits, 124
salad, 26-7, 46-56, 65-6
sandwiches, hot grilled, 80
savoury tchease spread, 83
scones, hot peanut butter, 26-7
shortcake, strawberry, 144-5
sladké knedlíky, 118-19
sorbets, 107-8
soufflés, 33, 91
soups, 36-45
soy sauce, 19-20
soya milk, 19
soya yogurt, 21-2

spinach: spinach noodle bake, 86
  spinach soufflés, 91
spread, savoury tchease, 83
strawberries: strawberry and almond ice-cream, 106
  strawberry shortcake, 144-5
sugar, 10
SuperSpread, 12, 19
sweet potatoes and plums, 92
sweeteners, 10
sweets, 125-7
Syrian date crescent pastries, 128-9

tamale pie, hot, 76-7
tarts, 132-5
tchease spread, savoury, 83
teabreads, 141-3
Three Nut Butter truffles, 125
tofu: savoury tchease spread, 83
  smoked tofu with barbecue sauce, 88-9
tomatoes: organic cream of tomato soup, 39
  tomato and bean soup, 42
truffles, Three Nut Butter, 125
Turkish-style helvah, 127

vegan diet, 16
Vegeburger mix, quick chilli, 79
vegetables: oil-free stir-fried vegetables, 89
  side dishes, 90-9
  spicy vegetable cocktail, 149
  ten-minute vegetable stew Italiano, 77

walnuts: plum and walnut bread, 141
  walnut and caper rice salad, 49

yogurt: raspberry and apricot frozen yogurt parfaits, 109
  soya yogurt, 21-2